The Japanese Banking Crisis

"Himino Ryozo has provided analysis of the 97-98 Japanese banking crisis that is clear, concise and compelling. Himino-san examines the causes, consequences and – most importantly – the lessons learnt from a traumatic period in Japanese financial history. He does so with the benefit of a career spent at the forefront of financial policy-making, both in Japan and internationally.

It is often said 'History doesn't repeat itself, but it often rhymes.' Many attributes of the Japanese banking crisis have, at their heart, difficult choices, missed opportunities and occasional failings that are in no way unique to Japan. Himino-san's examination of the Japanese crisis should therefore be valued reading not just for Japanese policymakers, but financial policymakers the world over. Financial crises are all-too-frequent, and extremely costly. This analysis provides useful insights as to how we might do better to reduce and combat the crises of the future."

—Wayne Byres, *Chair, Australian Prudential Regulation Authority*

Himino Ryozo

The Japanese Banking Crisis

Himino Ryozo
Financial Services Agency
Tokyo, Japan

ISBN 978-981-15-9597-4   ISBN 978-981-15-9598-1 (eBook)
https://doi.org/10.1007/978-981-15-9598-1

© The Editor(s) (if applicable) and The Author(s) 2021. This book is an open access publication.
Open Access This book is licensed under the terms of the Creative Commons Attribution-NonCommercial-NoDerivatives 4.0 International License (http://creativecommons.org/licenses/by-nc-nd/4.0/), which permits any noncommercial use, sharing, distribution and reproduction in any medium or format, as long as you give appropriate credit to the original author(s) and the source, provide a link to the Creative Commons license and indicate if you modified the licensed material. You do not have permission under this license to share adapted material derived from this book or parts of it.
The images or other third party material in this book are included in the book's Creative Commons license, unless indicated otherwise in a credit line to the material. If material is not included in the book's Creative Commons license and your intended use is not permitted by statutory regulation or exceeds the permitted use, you will need to obtain permission directly from the copyright holder.
This work is subject to copyright. All commercial rights are reserved by the author(s), whether the whole or part of the material is concerned, specifically the rights of translation, reprinting, reuse of illustrations, recitation, broadcasting, reproduction on microfilms or in any other physical way, and transmission or information storage and retrieval, electronic adaptation, computer software, or by similar or dissimilar methodology now known or hereafter developed. Regarding these commercial rights a non-exclusive license has been granted to the publisher.
The use of general descriptive names, registered names, trademarks, service marks, etc. in this publication does not imply, even in the absence of a specific statement, that such names are exempt from the relevant protective laws and regulations and therefore free for general use.
The publisher, the authors and the editors are safe to assume that the advice and information in this book are believed to be true and accurate at the date of publication. Neither the publisher nor the authors or the editors give a warranty, expressed or implied, with respect to the material contained herein or for any errors or omissions that may have been made. The publisher remains neutral with regard to jurisdictional claims in published maps and institutional affiliations.

Cover credit: © Melisa Hasan

This Palgrave Macmillan imprint is published by the registered company Springer Nature Singapore Pte Ltd.
The registered company address is: 152 Beach Road, #21-01/04 Gateway East, Singapore 189721, Singapore

Contents

1	**Introduction**	1
	Financial Cycle and Business Cycle	2
	Learning from Mistakes	5
	Five Phases in the Japanese Financial Cycle of 1986–2004	6
	References	7
2	**Bubbles**	9
	Export-Led Growth Strategy Reaching an Impasse	10
	Expanding Domestic Demand	11
	Financial Deregulation	14
	Bankers' Existential Threat	16
	Bubbles	19
	What Japan Gained and Lost	22
	References	25
3	**Pricking Bubbles**	27
	Monetary Policy	28
	Prudential Policy	29
	Tax, Land, and Fiscal Policies	33
	Clean or Lean?	34
	Too Little, Too Late?	36
	In Hindsight	42
	References	44

4 In-Between Years 47
Estimating the Size of the Problem 48
Catch 22 50
The Finance Ministry's Choice 52
The Bank of Japan and the Prime Minister 54
Orderly Resolution Without Bailout 56
References 60

5 Crisis 63
Political Leadership 64
Capital Injections and Raids on Regulators 65
Summer 1998 66
Evolution of Resolution Approaches 69
Disclosure, Provisioning, and Corrective Actions 70
New Supervisory Culture 72
Credit Crunch, Recession, Bankruptcy, Unemployment, and Suicide 74
Moral Hazard and Firefighting 77
References 80

6 Restructuring Banks and Borrowers 83
Resolving Bad Loans 85
Resolving Banks 89
Restructuring Borrowers 90
Labor Market Adjustments 95
How Much Did It Cost? 97
What if the Immediate Clean-Up Option Had Been Chosen in 1992? 99
References 102

7 What Japan Gained and Lost 105
References 115

Index 117

ABOUT THE AUTHOR

Himino Ryozo is the commissioner of the Financial Services Agency (JFSA), Japan's integrated financial regulator, and the chair of the Financial Stability Board's Standing Committee on Supervisory and Regulatory Cooperation (SRC), a global forum of regulatory authorities, central banks, finance ministries, and international standard setting bodies. At the Agency, he supervised banks, insurers, broker dealers, and audit firms and regulated capital markets during the last two decades. He also served as the secretary general of the Basel Committee on Banking Supervision from 2003 to 2006 and helped the Committee finalize the Basel II capital adequacy standards. He graduated from the University of Tokyo (LL.B.) and Harvard Business School (MBA).

List of Figures

Fig. 1.1	A stylized mechanism of the financial cycle	3
Fig. 1.2	Business cycles and financial cycles in Japan	4
Fig. 2.1	Bank loans relative to GDP	17
Fig. 2.2	Sectoral net land purchases and land price	20
Fig. 2.3	Balance sheet of the real estate sector	21
Fig. 2.4	National capital gain/loss relative to GDP	22
Fig. 3.1	Banks' lending attitude to the real estate and manufacturing industries	32
Fig. 3.2	Policy rates and real estate prices in Japan and the United States	38
Fig. 3.3	Actual policy rates compared with Taylor targets	40
Fig. 5.1	Bankruptcy, unemployment, and suicides	76
Fig. 6.1	Persistent vicious cycle	84
Fig. 6.2	Bad loans held by banks and loan losses incurred	87
Fig. 6.3	Composition of the loans categorized doubtful or worse and removed from the balance sheets of major banks	95
Fig. 6.4	Corporate non-recurring profit/loss and credit cost to banks	98
Fig. 7.1	Financial surplus/deficit of private non-financial corporates	106
Fig. 7.2	Balance sheet composition of private non-financial corporations	107

Fig. 7.3   Factor contributions to the potential growth rate   108
Fig. 7.4   Changes in the economic clout of countries and the living standard of nationals   109
Fig. 7.5   Changes in real GDP per capita   111
Fig. 7.6   Male and female life expectancy at birth in Germany, Japan, and the United States   114

LIST OF TABLES

Table 3.1	Guidance issued by the Ministry of Finance and the Bankers' Association	30
Table 3.2	Supervisory guidance issued by US authorities	41
Table 4.1	In-between years in major banking crisis episodes since 1990	48
Table 4.2	Non-performing loan amounts estimated in 1992	50
Table 5.1	Evolution of resolution approaches	70

CHAPTER 1

Introduction

Abstract Since the mid-1980s, Japan, which was a leading competitor in the world's manufacturing sector, tried to transform itself to an economy with domestic demand-led mature growth. The ensuing bubbles, busts, and banking crisis, however, left the country chronicle deflation and stagnation. This book analyzes why the Japanese authorities could not avoid making choices that led to this outcome.

Keywords Financial cycle · Business cycle · Learning lessons · Greek tragedies · Déjà vu · Bubbles · Forbearance · Banking crisis · Clean-up

This report describes policy responses to the boom, bust, crisis, and recovery Japan experienced during the two decades from 1986 to 2004.

One hundred and fifty years ago, Japan started to westernize itself after the two centuries of isolation. Since then, it has made two miracles and two major mistakes.

The first miracle was the rapid modernization which within half a century turned the small agricultural island country in the eastern end of Asia into one of the five powers of the world. The miracle ended by the first tragic mistake of engaging in the Second World War. The US air raids in 1945 demolished the country.

The second miracle was its resurrection from ashes and the ensuing rapid economic growth. The country by 1968 became the second-largest economy in the world and dominated the world's manufacturing markets one by one; first textile, then steel, electronic appliances, automobiles, machine tools, and semiconductors. At the end of 1989, Japan was the world's largest creditor country. The eight largest banks in the world were all Japanese. The Tokyo Stock Exchange had the largest market capitalization and the Osaka the third largest. In 1995, the economic size of the archipelago reached 71% of that of the United States. Compare this with the relative size of the Chinese economy in 2018 to the US one: 66%.[1]

This report is about the second tragic mistake which brought Japan from a leading economic power into an economy which struggled with persistent deflation and stagnation. It tries to explore where things went wrong, what were the alternatives, how and why the choices were made, and what would be needed to do better in the future.

Financial Cycle and Business Cycle

The protagonist of the report is the financial cycle, or the financial boom-and-bust cycle. Figure 1.1 describes its stylized mechanism. In a market upturn, hikes in asset prices, increased collateral values, higher bank profits, reduced risk perception, and lax underwriting standards come hand in hand. These often result in over-investment, overspending and, eventually, build-up of unsustainable projects and overextended borrowers.

At the moment investors realize that the assets which looked like gems are in fact garbage—the Minsky moment, so dubbed in praise of Hyman Minsky's work in the 1970s—asset prices collapse, liquidity dries up, banks realize losses, capital constraints create a credit crunch, and the effects feed through to the real economy. Eventually, there is a reverse Minsky moment, when at the current market prices the assets once again look like good bargains.

The financial cycle tends to last longer than the business cycle. Borio (2014) argues that the business cycle typically ranges from 1 to 8 years, while the average length of the financial cycle has been around 16 years. That has indeed been the case in Japan, as Fig. 1.2 shows.

1 INTRODUCTION

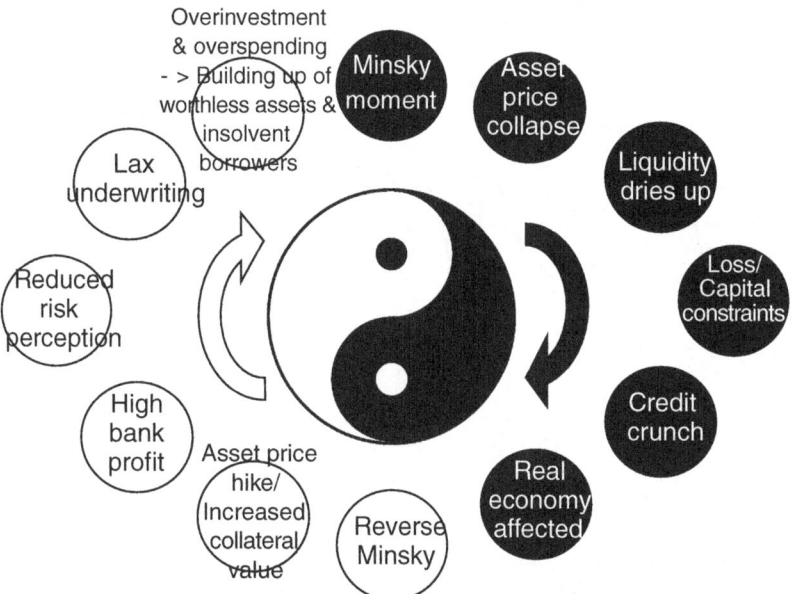

Fig. 1.1 A stylized mechanism of the financial cycle (*Source* Himino [2009] at Risk.net)

Before the financial deregulation of the 1980s, advanced economies seldom encountered financial crises. At that time, economic policymakers in the advanced economies could largely forget about financial cycles and just focus on business cycles. After a decade in the job, they could acquire full knowledge of their trade through their own experience.

But since the financial deregulation of the 1980s, financial crises have become "an equal opportunity menace" for both advanced and emerging economies (Reinhart and Rogoff 2009). In order to witness all phases of a financial cycle, one needs to devote almost a full professional working life: For example, since I became a financial regulator 37 years ago, I have witnessed six-and-a-half business cycles in Japan, but only two-and-a-half financial cycles. One's own experience therefore would not suffice. Those responsible for the financial stability or the macroeconomic policy need to learn from both other jurisdictions and history. Hence, the value of adding a concise overview of the Japanese case to policymakers' library.

Panel A. Business cycles in Japan

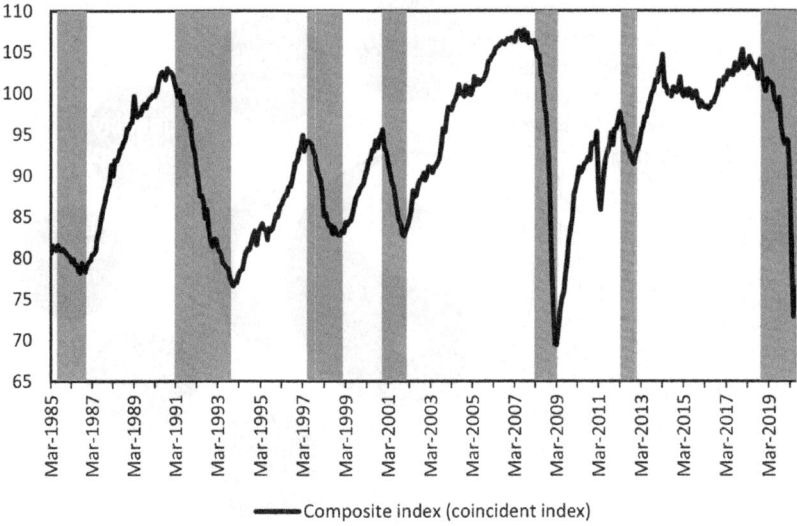

Panel B. Financial cycles in Japan

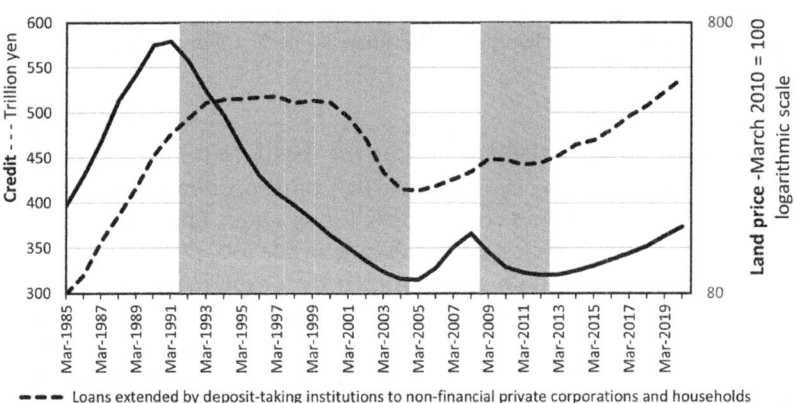

Fig. 1.2 Business cycles and financial cycles in Japan (*Note* The unshaded areas indicate upturns and the shaded areas represent downturns. *Source* Cabinet Office, The Reference Dates of Business Cycle, and Index of Business Conditions; Bank of Japan, Flow of Funds Accounts Statistics; and Japan Real Estate Institute, Urban Land Price Index)

Learning from Mistakes

When we try to learn from our own mistakes, we typically identify immediate and root causes and remove or mitigate them. If the mistakes are others', we identify why they went wrong and work to avoid doing the same. If that were enough, however, financial crises would not have been repeated so often.

We make many minor mistakes due to carelessness, stupidity, or greed. But, as classical Greek tragedies well portray, we make major mistakes because we are driven by forces bigger than us. Many people work with all their might and in good faith, but sometimes the combined effects of such efforts lead us to a tragedy. Only by understanding such mechanisms, can one avoid another tragedy.

Many of the English-language resources attribute what happened in Japan to incompetence or insincerity of policymakers, and perverse and outdated systems and practices unique to Japan. Those analyses helped the Japanese policymakers correct their deficiencies but may have nurtured a sense of complacency among non-Japanese people that similar crises would never happen outside of Japan.

Many incidents in the Global Financial Crisis in the 2000s, however, gave those who lived through the Japanese crisis a sense of déjà vu. The sudden market gridlock in the wake of the collapse of Lehman Brothers in 2008 resembled the interbank market freeze after the failure of the Sanyo Securities in 1997. Secretary Paulson's "Super SIV" proposal in 2007 was reminiscent of the Japanese Cooperative Credit Purchasing Corporation established in 1993. Depositors' long queues at Northern Rock branches in UK looked like what the Japanese saw across the country on November 26, 1997. The standoff over the Troubled Asset Relief Program at the US parliament in September 2008 revoked the memory of the debate over the bills on bank resolution at the Japanese Diet in August 1998.

To avoid repeating what Japan did, we need to know why it was hard for the Japanese policymakers at the time to make different choices.

Five Phases in the Japanese Financial Cycle of 1986–2004

In the following chapters, policy responses to the Japanese financial cycle of 1986–2004 are described in five phases.

The first phase is the build-up of the asset price bubbles and corporate debts in 1986–1990. Chapter 2 will discuss how the fear of the trade war and the dream of a global city fueled the asset price booms. It will also discuss the relationship between the financial deregulation and the deterioration in the lending standards.

The second phase is the peaking of the bubbles between 1990 and 1991. As Galbraith (1954) said, "A bubble can easily be punctured. But to incise it with a needle so that it subsides gradually is a task of no small delicacy." Did the Japanese authorities do too little and too late? Was the behavior of the US authorities in the 2000s any different? These are the questions I will try to answer in Chapter 3.

The third phase is the long intermission between 1990 and 1997. In most other cases, the periods between the asset price peaks and the systemic banking crises lasted only one to three years. But in Japan's case, the intermission lasted as long as seven years. Chapter 4 will discuss whether the long intermission was the result of forbearance which exacerbated the problem or the inevitable result of lacking powers and funding to implement orderly resolutions.

The fourth phase is the systemic banking crisis in late 1997 and 1998. Crisis management requires considerations distinct from those needed in times of calm. Chapter 5 will discuss the tradeoff between preventing moral hazard and firefighting.

The fifth phase is the balance sheet adjustment of banks and borrowers between 1999 and 2004. The clean-up done during the period finally restored financial stability but at the same time made the whole Japanese economy more risk averse. Chapter 6 discusses this.

Chapter 7 reviews what Japan gained, kept, and lost during the two decades.

Books and articles written in Japanese and not translated in English are listed in the Reference section with the titles I have provisionally translated into English, together with the phonetic representation of the original Japanese title. Quotes from them are also translated by me. A Japanese name is expressed in the Japanese style (the family name followed by the given name, e.g., Ono Yoko), not in the Western style (Yoko Ono).

A Japanese fiscal year starts in April of the year and end in March in the next year. For example, FY 2020 refers to the period between April 2020 and March 2021.

The chapters are based on a series of lectures to regulators from emerging economies delivered at the Global Financial Partnership Center of the Financial Services Agency of Japan (JFSA) and benefitted from conversations with them. Wayne Byres gave this plain book beautiful words of recommendation. Amaya Tomoko, Hayasaki Yasuhiro, Himino Sumako, Hirabayashi Takaaki, Ito Yutaka, Nishida Yuuki, Tsubouchi Hiroshi, Ueda Kenichi, and Yoshida Akihiko reviewed drafts and gave invaluable comments. Jacob Dreyer and Anushangi Weerakoon of Palgrave Macmillan and Arun Kumar Anbalagan and Keerthana Muruganandham of Springer Nature provided professional editorial support. I would like to thank them all.

The views expressed are mine and are not meant to represent the views of the organizations I am affiliated with.

Note

1. World Bank, World Development Indicators database.

References

Borio, C. (2014). The financial cycle and macroeconomics: What have we learnt? *Journal of Banking & Finance, 45*, 182–198.
Galbraith, J. K. (1954). *The great crash 1929*. Boston: Houghton Mifflin.
Himino, R. (2009). A counter-cyclical Basel II. *Risk, 22*(3), 72–74.
Reinhart, C. M., & Rogoff, K. S. (2009). *This time is different: Eight centuries of financial folly*. Princeton: Princeton University Press.

Open Access This chapter is licensed under the terms of the Creative Commons Attribution-NonCommercial-NoDerivatives 4.0 International License (http://creativecommons.org/licenses/by-nc-nd/4.0/), which permits any noncommercial use, sharing, distribution and reproduction in any medium or format, as long as you give appropriate credit to the original author(s) and the source, provide a link to the Creative Commons license and indicate if you modified the licensed material. You do not have permission under this license to share adapted material derived from this chapter or parts of it.

The images or other third party material in this chapter are included in the chapter's Creative Commons license, unless indicated otherwise in a credit line to the material. If material is not included in the chapter's Creative Commons license and your intended use is not permitted by statutory regulation or exceeds the permitted use, you will need to obtain permission directly from the copyright holder.

CHAPTER 2

Bubbles

Abstract In the latter half of the 1980s, Japan's export-led growth strategy reached an impasse. To avoid a trade war with the United States and to stop the hyper-appreciation of the yen, it tried to rectify its trade imbalance by stimulating domestic demands. The country also embarked on financial deregulation. These resulted in asset price bubbles, which was much bigger than the ones in the United States in the 2000s.

Keywords Export-led growth · Trade war · Strong yen · Domestic demand · Global city · Monetary policy · Fiscal policy · Deregulation · Bubbles

By the mid-1980s, the Japanese economy had overgrown the limit its export-led growth strategy could sustain economically and geopolitically. In his analysis of fault lines leading to financial crises, Rajan (2011) argued, "What is particularly alarming for the future of countries following this path [of dependence on exports for growth] is that Japan did try to change, but without success." In this chapter, we look at how Japan tried to transform itself, and how the efforts, combined with the universal mechanism of financial cycles, drove the country from despair in 1986 to lethal hubris in 1989.

Export-Led Growth Strategy Reaching an Impasse

The export-led growth strategy, which led Japan to become the second-largest economy in the world, reached an impasse by the mid-1980s. Two symptoms signaled that Japan had overgrown its strategy: the trade war with the United States and the rapid appreciation of the yen.

In 1985, the US Senate passed by 92-0 a resolution urging the US president to retaliate against Japanese imports. That same year, Prime Minister Nakasone urged the nation to buy 100 dollars more per person of foreign products. In 1986, former foreign minister Okita, after having visited Washington, DC, reported back to Tokyo that the atmosphere there was like that on the eve of the outbreak of war.

In April 1987, the US president decided to apply retaliatory tariffs on imports from Japan. In May, the US House of Representatives overwhelmingly approved a trade bill which included retaliatory provisions targeted at Japan. In July, seven US congressmen invited journalists to a courtyard at Capitol Hill, where they smashed with hammers electronic appliances made in Japan. The scene was broadcast and shocked the Japanese. The ratio of Americans who responded yes when asked if Japan is a dependable friend declined from 57% in 1984 to 48% in 1988.

Throughout the post-WWII period, the Japan–US relationship was the cornerstone of the Japanese diplomacy. The United States was by far Japan's largest trading partner; and Japan relied on US troops stationed in Japan, the Seventh Fleet of the US Navy, and US nuclear deterrence for its national security. A trade war with the United States had to be averted at any cost.

The second symptom was the rapid appreciation of the yen.

Japanese industry and government initially considered acquiescing on the appreciation of the yen if such a move would alleviate the risk of a trade war. Paul Volcker recounts that, at the meeting of the Group of Five finance ministers and central bank governors on September 22, 1985, he was startled to see that the Japanese finance minister Takeshita was far more forthcoming than other participants had expected and volunteered to permit the yen to rise by more than 10%.[1] The meeting produced the Plaza Accord, which stated that "some further orderly appreciation of the main non-dollar currencies against the dollar is desirable."

The ensuing appreciation of the yen was by no means orderly and was far beyond the initial anticipation. The yen, which was at 240 yen per dollar on the Friday before the Sunday Accord, reached 152 yen per dollar one year later, and 121 yen per dollar at the end of 1987, doubling its value against the dollar just within two-and-a-quarter years. Japanese manufacturers were thrown into a panic. They repeatedly introduced aggressive cost reduction plans, only to be defeated by the new exchange rate.

Halting the appreciation of the yen thus became the top priority of Japan's economic policy. Miyazawa Kiichi, who succeeded Takeshita as finance minister, later recounted, "When I became finance minister in July 1986, the minister's job was nothing other than to think about how to excuse the endless yen appreciation and what the government could do to address it."[2] Sumita Satoshi describes his term as the Bank of Japan governor (1984–1989), "From the beginning to the end, it was about the exchange rates."[3]

Expanding Domestic Demand

To address the risk of a trade war and the appreciation of the yen, Japan mobilized a whole range of policy tools, including a new national doctrine to transform the economic structure, government-designed dreams and projects, deregulation of land use, and fiscal and monetary stimulus.

The prime minister asked Mayekawa Haruo, a former governor of the Bank of Japan, to chair a wise men's group, the Committee on Structural Adjustment of the Economy for International Coordination, and find solutions. The report by the Committee published in 1986, or the Mayekawa Report, was ready to sacrifice even the lifestyle of the nation for international coordination:

> Japan's long-lasting large-scale current account imbalance is driving both the Japanese economic policy and the harmonious development of the global economy into a crisis. Now it is the time for Japan to make a historic transformation of its economic policy and of the lifestyle of the nation.

To attain "the transformation into the domestic-demand driven and international-coordination oriented economic structure," the report provided a list of recommendations. The top item on the list was the expansion of domestic demand.

One week after the publication of the report, Prime Minister Nakasone flew to Washington, DC and presented it to President Reagan.

Later, Prime Minister Takeshita, who succeeded Nakasone, incorporated the recommendations into his five-year economic plan titled *Japan in Symbiosis with the World*. Domestic demand-led growth had become a new national doctrine, replacing that of export-led growth.

The quickest means of expanding domestic demand is boosting public works, but, as the government had the policy of achieving fiscal consolidation without tax increases, it decided to rely on the mobilization of private sector funds for large-scale projects by way of policy inducements. The policy was called *min-katsu*, where *min* stood for private sector funds and *katsu* for mobilization.

The government started massive sales of state-owned land to the private sector for use in development projects. A special *min-katsu* law was enacted to introduce a package of deregulations. These policies were accompanied by the government-created visions of a global city and resort towns.[4] The Fourth National Comprehensive Development Plan, approved by the cabinet in February 1987, maintained, "The Tokyo area is expected to accumulate global-city functions such as those of international financial and information hub and will become the core city of the Pan-Pacific region and one of the nerve centers of the world." It predicted that additional 4000 hectares of office space, or office space equivalent to that which already existed in central Tokyo, would be needed in the wider Tokyo region by 2000.

National ministries and agencies, local governments, and industry rushed into the competition to lead new projects. When the Tokyo Metropolitan Government presented a project to develop an area near Tokyo Bay in 1985, the size of the project was only 40 hectares, but the next year, the joint statement by seven ministries and agencies expanded it to 1200 hectares. Gigantic projects designed by the public sector strengthened the bullish sentiments in the society at the time, but the projects themselves mostly ended up with bankruptcies later.

Often government-invented visions are forgotten soon after their heralded announcement, but, for good or bad, the vision of the global-city Tokyo was widely believed in and actively utilized. A popular movie produced in 1988, *Tax Investigation Woman 2*, depicted an underworld figure who assimilated his mission with the nation's future. He recounts, "We kick and scare current residents out of building sites for the sake of the country. For Tokyo to become an international information hub and a global financial center, we need to attract big businesses from around the world. However, office space is absolutely in shortage. If we do not do land sharking, then Hong Kong will immediately take over Tokyo's potential role."

In retrospect, the prediction presented in the Fourth National Comprehensive Development Plan was not off the mark. In 2000, the total area of the office space in central Tokyo doubled to 8000 hectares, and the vacancy rate was in line with the natural vacancy rate. Tokyo failed to become a top-tier global financial center, but we cannot blame planners in 1987 for not being able to predict the calamities happened in Japan in the 1990s. Perhaps the problem was not the vision itself but the way it was utilized to justify reckless projects and lending.

For regions outside Tokyo, the government coined another vision: The Japanese had overworked in the past but, having become rich, they would spend their leisure time on golfing or ski runs in resort towns. In 1987, the Resort Development Law was enacted.

Development projects pursued in line with this vision included the world's largest indoor beach designed to mimic Caribbean islands, the world's largest indoor skiing course, a world toilet museum exhibiting a pure-gold western-style toilet, a village imitating a Dutch town with a six-kilometer long canal, and a village which claimed to have imitated Turkey equipped with reconstructed Noah's Ark and a Trojan Horse.[5] The Japanese, however, took advantage of the strong yen and spent their leisure time in the real Caribbean islands rather than on the fake one, turning the latter into the world's largest indoor deserted beach.

The Bank of Japan aggressively eased its monetary policy. The official discount rate, which was 5% at the beginning of 1986, was reduced five times within two years to the historic low of 2.5% in February 1987 and stayed at that level for 2 years.

The chairman of the US Federal Reserve requested the Bank of Japan governor for a rate cut in August 1986, as did the US Treasury secretary to the Japanese finance minister in September.[6] In October, the secretary and the minister issued a joint statement and two days later the governor cut the rate from 3.5 to 3%. The statement of the Group of Six finance ministers and central bank governors, or the so-called Louvre Accord, of February 1987 characterized the cut to 2.5%, which was announced two days before the statement, as part of Japan's "monetary and fiscal policies which will help to expand domestic demand and thereby contribute to reducing the external surplus."

In May, the Japanese prime minister said to the US president that he had instructed the finance minister and the Bank of Japan governor on short-term interest rate and that the operation had commenced. The US president indicated his satisfaction.[7] Though the official discount rate stayed at 2.5%, the interbank market rate declined from 4% in March to 3.3% in May and stayed at the level during the summer. In June, on the margin of the G7 Summit meeting in Venice, the president stated to the prime minister that he hoped Japan to continue its efforts to lower interest rates and the prime minister responded that the efforts to guide short-term interest rates lower would be continued.[8]

As we will see in the next chapter, the Taylor rule, the monetary policy rule proposed by John Taylor in 1993, shows that the rate cuts during the period should have been even more aggressive than what the Bank of Japan did, given the strong deflationary impacts of the yen appreciation. In retrospect, it seems that the US authorities gave the right advice and that it was the Bank of Japan's failure to reverse the policy in 1988 that sowed the seeds of later problems.

Fiscal policy followed suit. In early 1987, the US president's decision to impose retaliatory tariffs on Japanese imports and the trade bill approved by the House shocked the Japanese government. The ruling party proposed a large fiscal stimulus package of 5 trillion yen and Prime Minister Nakasone increased it to 6 trillion. He reportedly said, "Hey, I had another go and beefed it up. The outcome is a significantly good one. The package will go a long way toward expanding domestic demand. I will attend the G7 Summit meeting in Venice with this policy package in hand. It will be appreciated."[9]

In Venice, the president told the prime minister that the United States would lift part of the sanctions on the semiconductor imports from Japan.[10]

Financial Deregulation

While the appetite for real estate investments and speculation was fueled by the whole array of policy packages, the bankers were stripped of the regulations which protected them from competition and constraints that they had been accustomed to living with for the preceding 40 years.

In 1984, deregulation was long overdue, given the emergence of the large government bond market, where interest rates were determined by supply and demand, and the growth in cross-border transactions with overseas markets, where deregulation had already advanced. Although Japan's financial system, which was designed to allocate resources according to industrial policies and development goals, proved to be highly efficient when the country was catching up with the United States and Europe, such a system might not be best suited to the post catch-up era, in which new frontiers of growth had to be explored on Japan's own, relying more on private sector entrepreneurship and innovation.

However, the move toward deregulation was initiated in the United States. In September 1983, Caterpillar Inc. published a report which argued that the company could not compete with Komatsu because the yen was unduly undervalued against the dollar and that the undervaluation was due to the highly regulated Japanese financial markets, which damaged the attractiveness of the yen. This theory of connecting trade competitiveness and financial deregulation should have been dubious at best, but, the next month, the Treasury Department was under fire within the US government for doing nothing on yen/dollar exchange rate issues.[11]

In February 1984, the US–Japan Ad Hoc Group on Yen/Dollar Exchange Rate was jointly established by the US Treasury and the Japanese Ministry of Finance, which at the time regulated and supervised the financial sector. At the joint meeting, directors general of the Ministry read out prepared statements one after another, listing reasons why the US requests could not be accommodated. Abhorred, the US side remarked that the Japanese responses were "formidable," but the word was lost in translation and some Japanese participants took it as praise.

The next month, the US Treasury secretary visited Tokyo to meet Japan's finance minister and expressed his frustrations with words and physical gestures undiplomatic enough to leave no room for misinterpretation. Two months later, the Ministry of Finance published its own report, and, on the same day, the Joint Ad hoc Group released a report which considerably overlapped with the Ministry's report.

As Kaminsky and Reinhart (1999) have shown, financial deregulation increases the risk of financial crisis across the world. The case of Japan was even more unfortunate, as Japan embarked on what it should have done on its own due to US demands rooted in dubious theory. It was not a helpful development in terms of fostering the Japanese people's propensity to think independently about their future and design their own financial system.

The Ministry knew that deregulation required effective supervision, proper market discipline, and a reliable safety net. The Ministry's 1984 report included plans to augment the disclosure requirements on banks and the deposit insurance system. Its 1985 report declared the need to strengthen its on-site inspection team.

The deregulation part of the plan was implemented as promised to the United States, but it was not easy to implement the plan to enhance the safety net, disclosure, or supervision. True, the Ministry did succeed in raising the deposit insurance limit from 3 to 10 million yen in 1986, despite the public opinion arguing rich people needed no protection. The Ministry also imported from the United States the purchase and assumption approach, a bank resolution method in which another bank purchases failed bank's assets and assumes its obligations with financial assistance provided by the resolution authority. To support purchase and assumption, the Deposit Insurance Corporation was given a power to make financial assistance within the limit of payout costs.

But the Deposit Insurance Corporation long stayed a paper company. The total number of its employees was 15 even in 1995. The banking industry repeatedly and successfully lobbied against the bills which intended to amend the Banking Law to strengthen disclosure requirements. Despite the Ministry's repeated pledge to augment its on-site inspection team, the number of inspectors at the headquarters grew from 76 in March 1984 only to 78 in March 1989, and the number at the local offices declined from 223 to 214.[12]

Before the deregulation, the Ministry was able to use its discretionary power to guide the industry and was considered highly influential. After the deregulation, however, it was left without means and tools to conduct effective supervision.

In both monetary policy and prudential policy, Japan initially resisted to the good advice given by the Unites States, then gave in, but failed to implement necessary follow-up measures—rate reversal in the case of monetary policy and enhanced supervision in the case of prudential policy—thereby sowing the seeds of future problem.

BANKERS' EXISTENTIAL THREAT

The banking industry was feeling an existential threat. After deregulations in the capital market, large corporates started to rely on bond issuance for funding and reduced their reliance on banks. In addition, due to the appreciation of the yen, the manufacturing industry, banks' traditional core customers, stopped constructing factories in Japan. On the other hand, bankers feared that deregulation of deposit interest rates would eventually work to raise banks' funding costs and limit lending margins.

Banks believed that, to survive, they should find new borrowers who were prepared to pay interests at higher rates. Bankers intensified their competition in lending to the real estate sector. Figure 2.1 shows how the banks compensated for the slowdown in lending to traditional borrowers

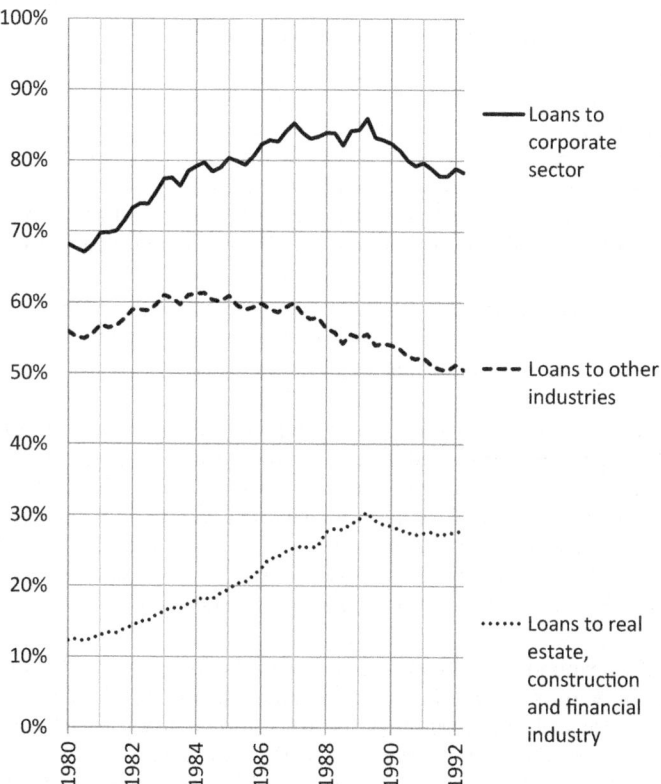

Fig. 2.1 Bank loans relative to GDP (*Source* Bank of Japan, Loans and discounts outstanding by industry; and Cabinet office, Annual Report on National Accounts of 2010—including retroactive results from 1980–)

by expanding their business with the real estate-related sectors, directly or via non-bank lenders.

The new business model did not look risky, as the Japanese land market had never experienced a period of declining prices after the World War II. Banks' profits surged. During the period, some Japanese banks weakened their traditional checking mechanisms by merging credit review departments with loan departments and by delegating more loan-approval powers from the headquarters to branches.

The following is a recollection on banking in the late 1980s that I heard in 1991 from a young banker at Mitsubishi Bank, which had the reputation of being the most conservative bank.

> I was a loan officer at a branch in Tokyo for three years. The branch had total outstanding loans of around 20 billion yen when I joined and 80 billion yen when I left. It may sound like a big surge, but the growth was slower than the growth at neighboring branches of other banks. We considered the nearby Sumitomo Bank branch as our rival and compared notes with it, but almost every month they wrote more in loans than us.
>
> The branch had about 20 loan officers. To compensate for the repayments of existing loans and to attain the net increase of 60 billion in three years, each officer had to write billions of yen in new loans per year.
>
> Even if I established a stronger relationship with one respectable medium-sized company and succeeded in raising Mitsubishi's share of that company's bank debt by 10 percent, the increase would be equivalent to only tens of millions of yen. To achieve the targeted increase in loans, I would have to do this for 100 customers a year. The bank's internal procedure for one lending decision would consume half a day of my time. I could not spend half a day for a loan of just tens of millions of yen.
>
> You are surrounded by colleagues who lend billions of yen at a time to someone who owns land. Some customers insist that they borrow money and provide collaterals, but that the bank should never pose questions on the use of funds or the business of the companies. In the freshman education course, you learn first that a bank is not a pawn shop, but if you do not act like a pawn shop, you will be left behind. I once lent two billion yen to such a customer with much fear and trembling, but later found out that a competitor had lent a much larger amount.

On top of the lending by banks' own branches, lending via non-bank lenders exploded during the period. The total outstanding loan amount of non-bank lenders jumped from 33 trillion yen, equivalent to 8% of bank loans, in March 1986 to 135 trillion yen, or 18%, in March 1991.

Some non-bank lenders were independent, but most were affiliated to one or more banks or insurance companies and borrowed from multiple banks and insurance companies. There were implicit assumptions that affiliated banks and insurance companies would step in if the lenders' business should go wrong, but the exact scope of responsibility was not stipulated. The non-bank lenders were not covered by the scope of direct supervision and inspection by the Ministry of Finance. This form of shadow banking resulted in business expansion without proper governance or supervision.

Bubbles

These moves triggered the classical mechanism of asset price bubbles common to any countries. Backed by growing demand, asset prices started to rise, collateral value increased, and banks' underwriting standards weakened. Credit expansion prompted speculative investments in land, and further increases in asset prices stimulated people's greed. The bullish sentiment prevailed in the Japanese society. But the degree of exuberance differed between the household, corporate, and banking sectors.

Between 1986 and 1991, corporations bought 13.4 trillion yen more in stocks than they sold, whereas households sold 14.6 trillion yen more than they bought.[13] Corporations bought, and households sold.

The pattern was similar but with a bigger scale in the case of land. During the same period, net purchases of land by non-financial corporations amounted to 60.5 trillion yen, financial institutions 18.7 trillion yen, general government 22.0 trillion yen, whereas households sold 102.5 trillion yen on net.[14]

Figure 2.2 shows the changes in land prices and the timing of purchase/sales by different sectors. As land prices went up, the households sold more and more, cashing in the capital gains, and the corporate sector bought more and more, sowing the seeds of future capital losses. In retrospect, it seems that households who sold high were wiser than businessmen who bought high. Unlike the US crisis in the 2000s that

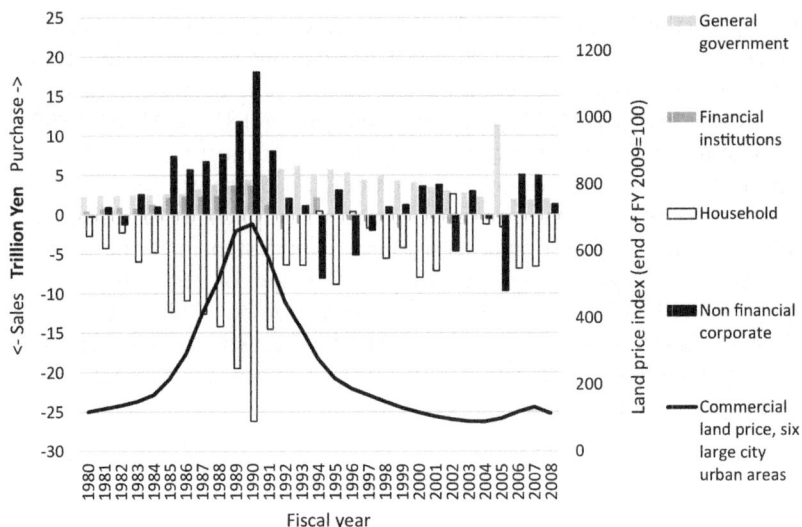

Fig. 2.2 Sectoral net land purchases and land price (*Source* Cabinet Office, Annual Report on National Accounts of 2010—including retroactive results from 1980—; and Japan Real Estate Institute, Urban Land Price Index)

was originated in household debt, the Japanese crisis in the 1990s was largely the problems of corporate borrowers.

Banks aggressively financed land purchases by corporations. As Fig. 2.3 shows, the size of the balance sheet of the real estate industry tripled between March 1986 and March 1992. The explosion was caused by a 56 trillion yen increase in real estate holdings on the asset side and a 64 trillion yen increase in borrowings from financial institutions on the liability side. Borrowings from financial institutions reached 94 trillion yen in March 1992, but the net worth, or the industry's own money available to cover losses before leaving losses to bankers, was as thin as 9 trillion yen.

Bankers' lending to the real estate sector became a major source of bad loans later.[15] The borrowers did not put much of their money at risk and the bankers relied on the real estate collateral that borrowers provided. However, when the borrowers' businesses went sour, the collateral also lost value. An example of wrong-way risk. The deal was for real estate companies to enjoy the capital gains should the land price go up, and for

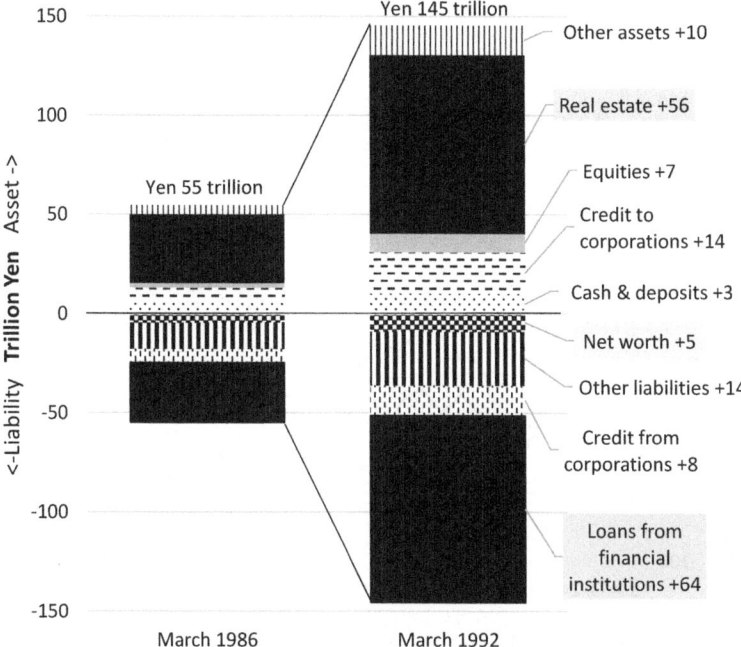

Fig. 2.3 Balance sheet of the real estate sector (*Source* Ministry of Finance, Financial Statements Statistics of Corporations by Industry)

bankers to absorb the capital losses should it go down. In retrospect, it seems that the real estate companies were wiser than the bankers.

The resultant asset price bubbles were enormous. The bubbles in Japan in the latter half of the 1980s were much bigger than those in the United States during the mid-2000s.

The size of the national capital gain in Japan during the 4-year period 1986–1989 was 4.8 times as large as its annual GDP, while that in the United States during the 4-year period 2003–2006 was only 1.6 times (Fig. 2.4).

In Japan, stock prices peaked at levels 3.0 times as high as pre-bubble, whereas in the US stocks peaked at only 1.5 times pre-bubble levels.[16] Japanese land prices rose 3.7 times higher in the latter half of the 1980s, whereas US home prices grew 1.7 times in the first half of the 2000s.[17]

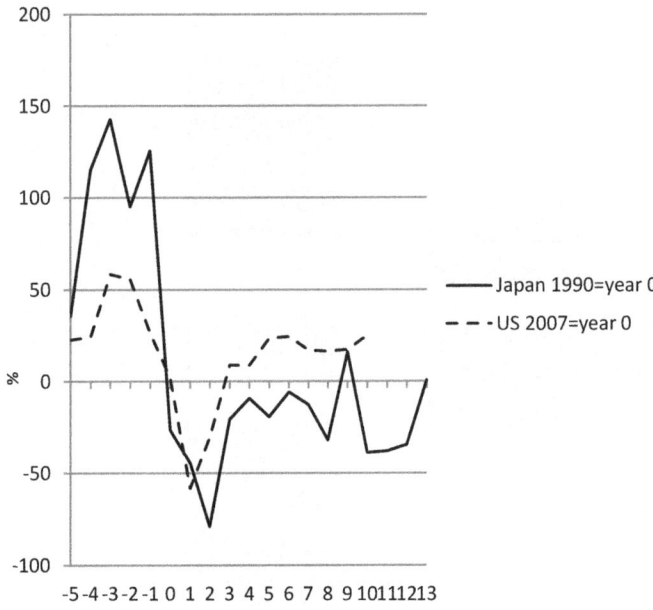

Fig. 2.4 National capital gain/loss relative to GDP (*Source* Cabinet Office, National accounts, integrated accounts, reevaluation accounts, changes in assets; and Bureau of Economic Advisors, Integrated macroeconomic accounts, Table S.2.a Selected Aggregates for Total Economy and Sectors, lines 1 & 62–67)

Although the exact numbers differ depending on the choice of indices and periods to compare, it may be said that the magnitude of the Japanese asset price bubbles was about two to three times as large as those in the United States. In addition, a significant part of the credit risk taken in the United States was transferred to Europe through the sales of subprime-loan backed securities and other instruments, while Japan largely absorbed the risk on its own.

What Japan Gained and Lost

At the end of 1989, Japan was the world's largest creditor country. The eight largest banks in the world were all Japanese. The Tokyo Stock Exchange had the largest market capitalization and the Osaka the third largest. Many believed in the valuation estimates that by selling the Imperial Palace site you could buy the whole land area of California, by selling the central part of Tokyo the whole United States, and by selling Japan you could buy the United States four times over.

Fear and despair in 1986 turned into hubris in 1989. With the emergence of windfall millionaires, national belief in the virtue of hard work and diligence was undermined. Some real estate developers paid handsomely to companies secretly affiliated with organized crime to kick residents out of building sites. The largest *yakuza* syndicate almost tripled its membership from 13,000 in 1985 to 35,000 in 1991.[18] The harm caused by bubbles was not limited to those on corporate and bank balance sheets.

Japan tried to transform itself from an export-led economy to a domestic demand-led one, rectify its trade imbalance, and avoid trade war and hyper-appreciation of the yen. The effort had enormous side effects, but did it at least attain the initial objectives?

Both Japan's bilateral trade surplus with the United States and its global trade surplus halved if measured in yen, and declined by 25% if measured in dollars.[19] Japan's net export to GDP ratio peaked in 1986 at 4% and declined to 1% in 1990. Japan's gross export to GDP ratio, which reached 14% in 1984, rapidly declined to 10% in 1987 and stayed at the level for more than a decade. We may say that the aim to rectify its major trade imbalance was attained.

The yen peaked at 121 yen per dollar in November 1988 and declined to 159 yen per dollar in April 1990. Strangely enough, however, the yen started to appreciate again as the Japanese economy got weakened by the collapse of the bubbles and surged as high as 81 yen per dollar in April 1995.

The relationship with the United States continued to deteriorate as the combination of the bubble economy and the appreciation of the yen inflated the optics of Japan's economic clout. Japan's GDP, which was only 31% of the US one in 1984, swelled to 71% in 1995.[20] In 1989, Sony acquired Columbia Pictures and Mitsubishi Real Estate bought Rockefeller Center. One of the founders of Sony and an influential member of the Diet jointly published a book titled *The Japan that can Say No* and proposed to use Japan's advanced technology as a source of military power. The title of the book sounded bold and rebellious, as it was taken for granted for many Japanese that Japan could never say no to any US requests. In 1990, Matsushita Electronics purchased Universal Pictures.

The sources of US concern on Japan proliferated from the trade issues to cultural invasion and national security. In 1989, the Atlantic Magazine, with the cover page depicting a giant sumo wrestler looking down at a small globe, carried a cover paper by James Fallows titled "Containing Japan," and the Newsweek magazine ran a front page with the picture of the Columbia lady wearing kimono and the caption "Japan Invades Hollywood." The 1992 novel by Michael Crichton *Rising Sun* and 1993 movie starring Sean Connery of the same title portrayed the criminal approach a fictitious Japanese company took to dominate American business and influence US politics.

The ratio of Americans who responded yes when asked if Japan is a dependable friend further declined from 48% in 1988 to 44% in 1990 and 1991. The ratio started to pick up in 1992 and reached 84% in 2011. By the time, after the two decades of economic stagnation, Japan had become insignificant as a potential competitor or a threat to the United States.

Notes

1. Volcker and Gyohten (1992).
2. Nihon Keizai Shinbunsha (2001).
3. Ibid.
4. For more on the harm of unfounded visions, see Yoshikawa (2001).
5. For photographs of these extraordinary projects, see Tsuzuki (2006).
6. Remarks of an anonymous high official of the Bank of Japan and an interview with Kiichi Miyazawa (Nihon Keizai Shinbunsha 2001).
7. Telegram from the ambassador to the United States to the minister of foreign affairs dated May 1, 1987 (R064534).
8. Telegram from the ambassador to Italy to the minister of foreign affairs dated June 9, 1987 (R085905).
9. NHK Shuzaihan (1996).
10. Telegram from the ambassador to Italy to the minister of foreign affairs dated June 9, 1987 (R085905).
11. For the detailed depiction of the interactions between the Japanese Ministry of Finance and the US Treasury, see Takita (2006).
12. Banking Bureau (1984) and (1989).
13. Stocks listed in the first section of the Tokyo Stock Exchange.
14. Cabinet Office, *National Account of 2008*.
15. In March 2002, 36% of major banks' non-performing loans were to the real estate industry and 25% of their lending to the real estate industry were non-performing (Bank of Japan 2002).

16. Nikkei Stock Price Index on December 29, 1989 compared with that on December 31, 1985 for Japan and Dow Jones Industrial Average in September 2007 compared with that in February 2003 for the United States.
17. Commercial land price index for six large cities in September 1990 compared with that in September 1985 for Japan and S&P/Case-Schiller 20-city Home Price in April 2006 compared with that in February 2003 for the United States. These indices were chosen as the commercial land price bubble was the key driver for the Japanese financial crisis whereas the residential real estate price bubble played the central role in the United States.
18. National Police Agency (2007).
19. Measured in yen, the bilateral surplus peaked at 9.4 trillion yen in 1985 and bottomed at 5.1 trillion yen in 1991, and the global surplus peaked at 14.2 trillion yen in 1986 and bottomed at 6.5 trillion yen in 1990. Measured in dollars, the bilateral surplus peaked at 57 billion dollars in 1987 and bottomed at 43 billion dollars in 1990, and the global surplus peaked at 92 billion dollars in 1988 and bottomed at 69 billion dollars 1990.
20. World Bank, World Development Indicators database.

References

Bank of Japan. (2002). *On the national banks' performance in the fiscal year 2001 (Zenkoku Ginkou no Heisei 13 nen'do Kessan ni tsuite)*.
Banking Bureau of the Ministry of Finance (Okurashou Ginkoukyoku). (1984). *The 33rd annual report of the Banking Bureau (Dai 33-kai Ginkoukyoku Kin'yuu Nenpou)*. Kin'yuu Zaisei Jijou Kenkyuukai.
Banking Bureau of the Ministry of Finance (Okurashou Ginkoukyoku). (1989). *The 38th annual report of the Banking Bureau (Dai 38 kai Ginkoukyoku Kin'yuu Nenpou)*. Kin'yuu Zaisei Jijou Kenkyuukai.
Kaminsky, G. L., & Reinhart, C. M. (1999). The twin crises: The causes of banking and balance-of-payments problems. *American Economic Review, 89*(3), 473–500.
National Police Agency. (2007). *The White Paper on Police 2007, Special feature: Choking off the financial sources of organized crime (Heisei 19-nen ban Keisatsu Hakusho, Tokyshuu: Bouryokudan no Shikin Choutatsu Katsudou tono Taiketsu)*. Gyousei.
NHK Shuzaihan. (1996). *NHK special, 50 years after the War, Japan at the moment, volume 6 (Sengo 50 nen Sono-toki Nihon ha dai 6 kan)*. Nihon Hoso Shuppan Kyokai.

Nihon Keizai Shinbunsha. (2001). *Reviewing bubbles; unintended errors (Kenshou Bubble, Han'i Naki Ayamachi)*. Nihon Keizai Shinbunsha.

Rajan, R. G. (2011). *Fault lines: How hidden fractures still threaten the world economy*. Princeton: Princeton University Press.

Takita, Y. (2006). *Japan-US negotiations on currencies, the true story told 20 years after (Nichibei Tsuuka Koushou, 20-nenme no shinjitsu)*. Nihon Keizai Shinbun Shuppan.

Tsuzuki, K. (2006). *The many faces of bubble (Baburu no Shouzou)*. Aspect.

Volcker, P. A., & Gyohten, T. (1992). *Changing fortunes: The world's money and the decline of American supremacy*. New York: Times Books.

Yoshikawa, H. (2001). Land bubbles—Causes and backgrounds (Tochi baburu—gen'in to jidai haikei), Chapter 9. In T. Muramatsu & M. Okuno (Eds.), *Studies on bubbles in Heisei-era, Book 1 (Heisei Baburu no Kenkyu Jou)*. Toyokeizai.

Open Access This chapter is licensed under the terms of the Creative Commons Attribution-NonCommercial-NoDerivatives 4.0 International License (http://creativecommons.org/licenses/by-nc-nd/4.0/), which permits any noncommercial use, sharing, distribution and reproduction in any medium or format, as long as you give appropriate credit to the original author(s) and the source, provide a link to the Creative Commons license and indicate if you modified the licensed material. You do not have permission under this license to share adapted material derived from this chapter or parts of it.

The images or other third party material in this chapter are included in the chapter's Creative Commons license, unless indicated otherwise in a credit line to the material. If material is not included in the chapter's Creative Commons license and your intended use is not permitted by statutory regulation or exceeds the permitted use, you will need to obtain permission directly from the copyright holder.

CHAPTER 3

Pricking Bubbles

Abstract In the late 1980s and early 1990s, Japan mobilized monetary, prudential, tax, land, and fiscal policy tools, first to moderate the appreciation of the yen, then to contain the land price bubble, and finally to mitigate the shock of the bust. This chapter reviews the timeliness and the calibration of the policy measures taken and attempt a comparison with the monetary and prudential policy measures in the United States in the 2000s.

Keywords Bubble buster · Quantitative restriction · Clean/lean · Too-little-too-late

In the late 1980s and early 1990s, Japan's policy priorities shifted from moderating the appreciation of the yen to containing the land price hike and then to mitigating the deflationary effects of the collapse of the bubbles. Monetary, prudential, tax, land, and fiscal policy measures were mobilized; first eased to mitigate the appreciation of the yen, then tightened to stop the land price hike, and eased again to accommodate the shock from the collapse of the bubbles.

Monetary Policy

For two years from February 1987 to May 1989, while the asset price bubbles continued to expand, the Bank of Japan kept its official discount rate at the post-war low of 2.5%.

The fear of strong yen prevented the Bank from tightening earlier. Sumita Satoshi, the governor of the Bank of Japan from 1984 to 1989, later recounted, "If we had tightened, the yen would have appreciated. . . . . The political sector, the industry, all were unanimous in demanding no stronger yen. Tightening was hard to do."[1] As soon as the yen plunged in May 1989, the Bank of Japan raised the rate.

The land price hike, which had been largely confined to Tokyo area, became a nationwide issue in 1989. The ratio of those who blame the government for its land and housing policy started to rise rapidly in late 1989. The public focus shifted from the yen to land. The "crazy land price" gave enormous windfall profits to landowners while depriving the dream to own a house from many, arousing a national anger.

Mieno Yasushi, who succeeded Sumita as the governor of the Bank of Japan in December 1989, stated at his inaugural press conference, "The nation is frustrated with the increasing wealth disparity among them resulting from the land and stock price boom." The finance minister demanded the governor to cancel the planned rate increase, but the governor did not take heed.

The Bank pursued tightening aggressively. It raised the rate three times in a half year, in May, October, and December 1989. Although the free fall in stock price commenced in January 1990, the Bank further raised the rate in March and August to 6%. The rate was increased five times within a year and three months, amounting to 350 basis point increase. The stock market continued to tumble, but the Bank kept the rate at 6% for almost a year.

Mieno was considered as a defender of central bank independence and a brave bubble buster. The public applauded him comparing him to a champion-of-justice *samurai*-police commissioner in eighteenth century Japan, the protagonist of a popular novel series.

The easing started only in July 1991, well after the stock price peak (December 1989), the six large city land price peak (September 1990), the inflation rate peak (December 1990), and the business cycle peak (February 1991), and slightly before the nationwide land price peak (September 1991). The minister for economic planning criticized the

Bank's tight monetary policy already in December 1990. Perhaps the minister knew better than the governor.

But at the time the Bank was largely surrounded by the hawkish public opinion. As late as in the autumn of 1991, major newspapers advocated, "Let's exterminate the land price bubble" (Asahi), "Bubble land prices shall not stay" (Mainichi), "Don't loosen land policy" (Yomiuri), "We cannot be relieved by moderated land prices" (Nikkei), and "Why rush to ease monetary policy?" (Tokyo).[2]

Ten years after, Ahearne et al. (2002), a team of economists at the US Federal Reserve Board, estimated that a further 200 basis point cut sometime between 1991 and early 1995 would have saved Japan from the chronic deflation, which haunted the country since the late 1990s. A Japanese politician gave an warning ten years earlier than them: Vice president Kanemaru of the ruling Liberal Democratic Party commented in February 1992 that, "even by chopping off the head of the Bank of Japan governor," a further 50 basis point cut had to be attained. One month later, the Bank reduced its policy rate by 75 basis points. It is said that the Bank had been in the process of a rate cut at the time of Kanemaru's remarks but that it chose to do so at a slightly different timing and size to protect the optics of central bank independence.[3]

The monetary policy moved largely in line with the shifts in public priorities from mitigating the strong yen, to containing the land price boom, and then to mitigating the effects of the bust. Governor Mieno, who took away the punch bowl while the party got going, was applauded as a champion of justice. When the effects of the land price bust manifested itself, however, the public changed their views and started to blame him for bringing in the crisis.

Prudential Policy

The Ministry of Finance, which then was the bank regulator, implemented from 1986 to 1989 a series of qualitative administrative guidance, gradually intensifying the measures (Table 3.1). In many other cases, guidance from regulators weaker than these had significant effects on the behavior of banks.[4] But the series of actions taken during the frenzy in the latter half of 1980s, even though they went as far as reporting requirements, interviews with aggressive banks, and on-site inspections, could not curb the financing of real estate investments.

Table 3.1 Guidance issued by the Ministry of Finance and the Bankers' Association

April 1986	Circular issued by the Ministry of Finance	Request to behave so as not to attract criticism that banks are encouraging speculative land deals Reporting requirements on land-related lending to real estate and construction industries
December	Circular issued by the Ministry of Finance	Request to strictly refrain from financing short-term resale of lands
July 1987	Extraordinary interviews conducted by the Ministry of Finance	Interviews on lending terms with banks making large amount of loans in regions showing conspicuous rise in land prices
	"Common understanding" published by the Bankers' Association	Confirmation that land-related lending attitude shall be strictly rectified
October	Circular issued by the Ministry of Finance	Request to be without flaws in not making loans to finance speculative land transactions Request to make sure that affiliated non-bank lenders shall do the same
	Bankers' Association's voluntary rules	Elimination of lending to finance speculative land transactions
October 1989	Circular issued by the Ministry of Finance	Expansion of the scope of extraordinary interviews Reporting requirements on lending to non-bank lenders Mobilize on-site inspections to contain lending to finance real estate speculations
March 1990	Circular issued by the Ministry of Finance	<u>Quantitative Restriction Circular</u>

Note The underlined measure is quantitative, while others are qualitative
Source Banking Bureau (1989, 1991)

However, the circular issued in March 1990 by the Ministry, or "the Quantitative Restriction Circular (QR)," made banks' real estate-related lending shut down abruptly.

The circular was a short, one-page document notifying the following two points:

i. For the time being, each bank shall restrain the growth of loans to the real estate industry so that it would not surpass the rate of growth of all loans.
ii. For the time being, reports on lending to the real estate and construction sectors and non-bank lenders shall be submitted to the Ministry.

The Ministry initially hesitated to use quantitative measures, which it considered as retrogressing back to the command and control days and being inconsistent with the deregulation approach it had pursued. Though the prime minister and the minister of the National Land Agency both intensified requests for quantitative measures from mid-1989, the Ministry continued to resist. But, when the land price data released in March 1990 revealed that the frenzy had spilled from Tokyo over to Nagoya and Osaka, the prime minister was angered and instructed the minister of finance to consider further measures. The Ministry finally changed its mind and later in the month issued the QR circular.[5]

In September 1990, or six months after the issuance of the circular, the land price index for six large cities peaked out. In September 1991, the land price index for regions other than the six large cities also peaked out. The Ministry of Finance requested the National Land Agency to conduct an extraordinary land price survey, confirmed that the prices were not rising, and lifted the QR in December 1991. The lifting was five months after the first reduction in the official discount rate by the Bank of Japan.

The 1990 QR circular was followed by the collapse of the real estate bubbles, while the series of circulars in the late 1980s seem to have had no noteworthy impacts. One possible reason of this difference may have been that the former was comprehensive in coverage (it covered all land-related loans, whether related to speculative activities or not) and its implementation was monitored quantitatively, while the latter were not. A former high official of the Ministry provides another explanation: "After all it was a matter of timing. The circular was issued right at the time when bankers started to think that they went too far and had piled on too much exposure. They noticed that they were in danger and started to run away from real estate related lending."[6]

Figure 3.1 shows survey responses of corporations in the real estate and manufacturing industries on banks' lending attitude to them. Tightening of banks' lending attitude to the real estate industry started a half year before the QR and at around the time of the first monetary policy tightening. The degree of the tightening, however, was far deeper for the real estate industry than for the manufacturing industry.

These may suggest that both the QR and the monetary policy affected the lending attitude. Perhaps the tightened monetary policy, bankers' growing awareness of their own excessive lending, and the QR reinforced each other and had unexpectedly strong aggregate effects.

Measures to contain bubbles tend to have bimodal effects: having no material impact or becoming a crashing blow. Multiple measures taken

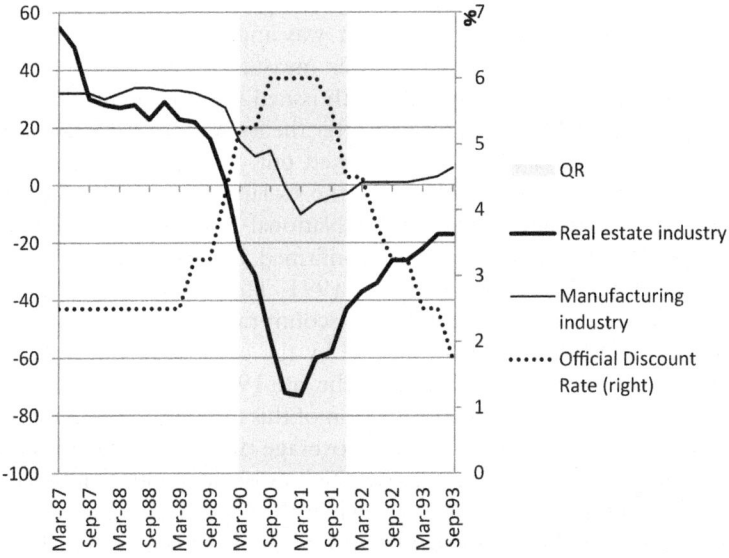

Fig. 3.1 Banks' lending attitude to the real estate and manufacturing industries (*Note* The level indicates the difference between the proportions of firms facing "easy" and "tight" bank lending attitude. Responses by companies of all sizes and on the current condition. *Source* The Bank of Japan, Short-term economic survey of enterprises [*Tankan* survey])

simultaneously may reinforce each other and have effects stronger than expected for each of the components.

The QR had stronger than anticipated effects, but it was hard to rescind it. As mentioned, even in autumn 1991, or right before the rescission, major newspapers were in unison in advocating extermination of the land price bubbles. According to another high official at the Ministry at the time, "My boss consulted me on lifting the QR. . . . I dissuaded him from trying it, saying that public opinion would beat us up and the lifting would not go through the necessary political process. My boss could not give up his idea and wished he could have found some means to achieve it."[7]

The public supported the introduction of the QR and criticized its lifting but turned to accuse the QR when the land price bust resulted in a recession. Tanizawa (1995), a renowned literary critic, wrote about the director general who issued the circular, "Given the enormous loss he inflicted to the nation, sawing, spearing, tearing, crucifying, burning, and boiling that criminal would not be enough." Apparently, he was not aware that it was the director general who most strongly resisted the political pressures demanding the QR and tried hard to rescind it as quickly as possible. A popular science fiction comedy film *Bubble Fiction: Boom or Bust* released in 2007 depicted a heroine who used a time machine to go back to 1990, fought with the wicked director general, and successfully blocked the QR. The heroine then returned to 2007 Japan and found the country in glittering prosperity after two decades of continued boom.

Tax, Land, and Fiscal Policies

In addition to monetary and prudential policies, tax and land policies were mobilized to contain the real estate boom.

Starting with the tax law amendments in September 1987, a series of measures were taken to tighten taxation on land capital gains and on the holding of land. Some of the measures were implemented with significant delay and should have worked to accelerate the land price collapse. For example, the Land-Holding Tax was implemented with the rate of 0.2% from January 1992, when the land prices were declining nationwide, and the rate was raised to 0.3% in 1993. It was maintained throughout the land price free fall until 1997, when the six-city area land price dropped to one quarter of the peak level. Another example was the appraised land prices for local tax on real estate holding: They long stayed far below the market prices but was raised dramatically in fiscal year 1993.

The land policy moved from gesture to action only after the peak. The National Land Utilization Law was amended in June 1987 to introduce a system of land price monitoring zones. Local governments were given the power to designate monitoring zones, advise suspension or alteration of particularly inappropriate transactions, and publish the names of those who did not abide by the advice. The power, however, was rarely activated, as it was difficult to determine which transaction was speculative and inappropriate.

The land policy's new objective, namely, "crash the land myth" (which meant ending the widely held belief that land prices never fall), was announced as late as in January 1991, when land prices of the six large city areas had already peaked out, and was maintained all through the land price free-falls, with various new measures added to increase the supply of land. For example, in 1992, when land prices were falling across the country, it was made easier to transform land from agricultural use to residential use. In the same year, new forms of land lease contracts were introduced to provide more flexibility in the land-supply modality. The "crash the land myth" banner was replaced with "enhance liquidity in the real estate market" only in 1997.

Fiscal policy was mobilized to mitigate the recession in the wake of the collapse of the bubble. In March 1992, the government published a stimulus package and announced that the implementation of the public works budgeted for fiscal year 1992 would be front-loaded. In August 1992, an additional stimulation package with a total expenditure amounting to 10.7 trillion yen, equivalent to 2% of the GDP, was announced. Further stimulation packages ensued.

CLEAN OR LEAN?

Should we prick the bubble in advance or focus on mitigating the shock of busts? Should we rely on monetary policy or resort to prudential policy? There has been a century long debate on these issues, and diverse, sometimes opposite, lessons have been drawn from each of major crisis episodes, including the Great Depression, the Japanese banking crisis, and the Global Financial Crisis.

There was a debate between the Federal Reserve Board in Washington, DC and the Federal Reserve Bank of New York in the late 1920s on how speculations in the stock market should be contained.[8] Washington was in charge of monetary policy, and did not want to use its own tool. It argued that, since the expected return on speculation was high, suppressing the speculations should require a massive policy rate increase, which would in turn halt sound productive activities. It wanted New York to do the job: Prudential policy tools (which then was called "direct pressure" on banks) could suppress speculations without damaging productive use of funds.

New York Fed, which was in charge of exerting direct pressure on banks, did not want to use its own tools either. It argued that, once member banks got the impression that they could not get money at any price, it might result in a critical situation. It wanted Washington to do the job: Speculative use of funds could not be distinguished from productive use, it was not possible to suppress only the former, and speculation could be contained only by monetary policy.

New York requested Washington to approve a discount rate increase for ten times, only to be rejected each time. The request was finally approved in August 1929, but the effect was mitigated by the reduction in bill rates, which was done to meet "productive fund demand."

The Black Monday and the Great Depression ensued. Two opposite lessons were drawn. Galbraith (1954) argued that the bubble should have been pricked decisively. According to him, Washington and New York avoided "an immediate and deliberately engineered collapse" and let a more serious disaster happen later on, because, (i) "a bubble can easily be punctuated" but "to incise it with a needle so that it subsides gradually is a task of no small delicacy," and (ii) someone would certainly be blamed for the ultimate collapse when it came anyway, but "there was no question whatever as to who would be blamed should the boom be deliberately deflated."

On the other hand, Bernanke (2002) considered that the Fed did too much to prick the bubble. Although "there was not the slightest hint of inflation," the Federal Reserve made "antispeculative" policy tightening and "the economy responded in the way that the monetary theory of the Great Depression would predict."

Similarly, Japan's bubbles and busts in the late twentieth century were interpreted in two opposite ways. At the Jackson Hall conference in 2003, Japan was named as a poster child of two opposing views.[9]

At the conference, Borio and White (2003), economists at the Bank for International Settlements, argued that monetary policy should be ready to lean against the build-up of financial imbalances even if near-term inflation pressures are not apparent. Responding to this, Michael Mussa, a former chief economist of the International Monetary Fund, commented, "It seems to me that the poster child for discussing why monetary policy should, in selected instances, pay serious attention to asset price distortions on the upside is not the United States in the late 1990s. It is Japan at the end of the 1980s.... Looking at a CPI inflation rate that remained very low saw an enormous explosion of asset prices, real estate prices, and enormous growth of credit. If that price bubble collapsed, there was going to be serious macroeconomic problems."

Ben Bernanke did not agree: "I am astonished by Michael Mussa citing Japan as a poster child for this paper. It is just the opposite.... The only place that monetary policy played a role was that in 1989 it intentionally tried to prick the bubble. It raised interest rates sharply in precisely the kind of program that is being suggested here. It did succeed in pricking the bubble. Asset prices collapsed and they had a 14-year depression."

After the Global Financial Crisis, the Cassandras who had warned against the build-up of financial imbalances strengthened their conviction. For example, White (2009) argue that the crisis demonstrated the need for monetary policy to focus more on "leaning" (i.e., preemptive tightening to moderate credit bubbles) than on "cleaning" (preemptive easing to deal with the after effects).

The main-stream view maintained its thrust after the crisis, but there have been some changes in nuances. The Federal Reserve acknowledged in its statement of longer-run goals and policy strategy in 2012 that the assessments of risks to the financial system was among the elements to be reflected in monetary policy decisions. The statement was amended in 2020 to place slightly more weights on a stable financial system, and an accompanying Q&A on the amendment recognized that risks to the financial system are an important factor in the monetary policy decisions.

Too Little, Too Late?

Today many believe that Japan's responses to the boom and the bust in the late 1980s and early 1990s were too little, too late, while the US responses in the 2000s were decisive and timely. Bernanke and Gertler (1999) and Okina et al. (2001) argue that the tightening to contain the bubbles should have started earlier, while Hamada et al. (2011) claim that the easing to mitigate the shock of the bust started too late. As already mentioned, Ahearne et al. (2002) argue that more aggressive easing after the collapse would have saved Japan from deflation.

Hamada et al. (2011) use the stock market price peak date as the benchmark in comparing the two episodes and argues, "In the US, the Federal Reserve Bank raised interest rates long before the stock market peaked, and cut rates very rapidly afterwards—indeed, had begun to cut before the peak. The Bank of Japan had been raising rates for some 18 months before the market peaked, and continued to raise them for over a year after the peak." The Federal Reserve appears to have behaved preemptively, while the Bank of Japan's behavior looks significantly belated.

But this comparison may entail two issues. First, the period between the start of the monetary policy tightening and the asset price peak may show how quickly the tightening (and other policy measures) worked, rather than how early the tightening started. We thus may want to look also at the period between the start of the bubbles and the start of the tightening. Second, the sequences of stock and real estate price peaks were reverse in the two episodes. In Japan, the stock price peaked nine months before the land price peak, while in the United States the real estate price peaked 18 months before the stock price peak.[10] As Crowe et al. (2014) explains, what matters most for financial stability is the real estate bubbles, not the stock price ones.

Figure 3.2 uses the real estate price peak dates, rather than the stock price ones, as benchmarks. To review the timeliness of the start of the tightening, it looks at the early periods of bubbles as well as the peak periods.

The start of the real estate price bubbles is difficult to discern in both cases. Shiller (2005) considers that the "rocket taking off" in the home price market was in 1998, while the first tightening was in June 2004. The period between the start of the bubbles and the start of the tightening was about six years.

As to Japan, the start of the real estate price bubbles seems to be somewhere between 1985 and 1987. (Yoshikawa [2002] regards 1985 as the first year of the land price bubbles. Figure 3.2 shows a land price kink in the latter half of 1986. Okina et al. [2001] considers 1987 as the start of the bubble period.) The first tightening was in May 1989. The period between the start of the bubbles and the start of tightening would then be two to four years, shorter in any way than the six years in the United States. This comparison may imply that the tightening in Japan started in an earlier phase in the formation of the bubbles than in the United States.

But an opposite conclusion can also be drawn. The US residential real estate price had risen by 20% during the year preceding the start

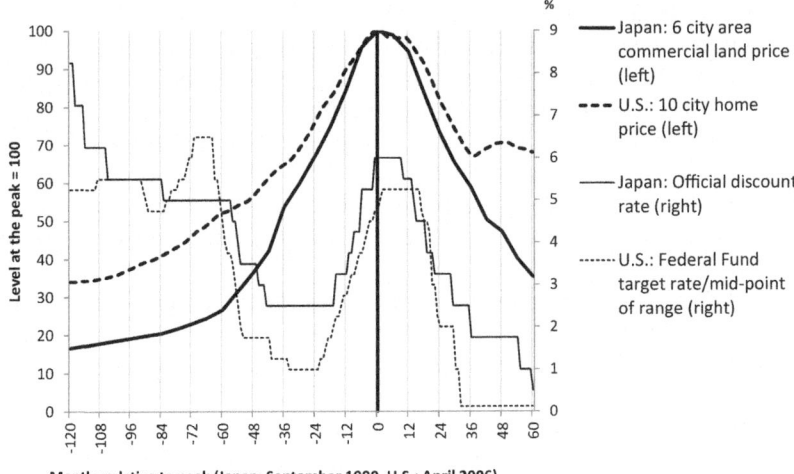

Fig. 3.2 Policy rates and real estate prices in Japan and the United States (*Source* Japan Real Estate Institute, Urban Land Price Index; S&P Dow Jones Indices LLC, S&P/Case-Shiller 10-City Composite Home Price Index; Bank of Japan, The Basic Discount Rate and Basic Loan Rate [Previously Indicated as "Official Discount Rates"]; and Board of Governors of the Federal Reserve System, Federal Funds Target Rate and Federal Funds Target Range)

of the tightening, up from the 13% rise during the year before that year. In Japan, the commercial land price had risen by 25% during the year preceding the start of the tightening, and the year before saw a 40% rise. This comparison would imply that Japan pushed down the brake pedal only after seeing an extreme exuberance, while the United States did so while the frenzy was still more moderate.

Was Japan later or earlier in starting the tightening? Figure 3.2 rather strikes us with similarity in the two episodes. In both episodes, the monetary policy was eased aggressively in the earlier phase of the real estate bubbles and was tightened pretty late in the cycle.

After the tightening, it took shorter period and smaller tightening to prick the bubbles in Japan than in the United States. The period between the start of the tightening and the real estate price peak was 16 months in Japan and 22 months in the United States. Japan tightened by 350 basis points and the United States by 425 basis points. Perhaps Japan saw the peak earlier with smaller tightening because (i) the frenzy was closer to the unsustainable level already at the time of the tightening and (ii) the QR brought forward the peak.

After the peak of the real estate prices, Japan started to ease a half year earlier but eased less aggressively than the United States. Japan started to ease 10 months after the real estate price peak, while the United States did so 17 months after. Japan eased by 225 basis points during the first year of easing, while the United States by 325 basis points; Japan by 350 basis points in the first two years, while the United States by 512.5 basis points.

In short, the trajectories of the monetary policies in the two episodes significantly resemble with each other throughout the cycle, with only minor differences in timing and calibrations.

One may say, however, that in measuring the degree of lean or clean, we should look at how much more the central banks did in addition to what was justified by the inflation and output condition at the time, rather than the absolute size of tightening and easing. Figure 3.3 compares the target rates suggested by the Taylor rule as proposed by Taylor (1993) (thin lines) and the actual policy rates (thick lines). Multiple target rates are shown using different estimates of the GDP gap.

Many believe that the Bank of Japan leaned to prick the bubble. But Japan did not lean more than the Taylor target. The Federal Reserve advocated that leaning was harmful and that cleaning after the bust was enough. The United States, however, did not clean more than the Taylor target. The major deviations in Japan from the Taylor target happened in 1986, when the easing was less aggressive than suggested by the rule. Perhaps if more had been done to mitigate the recession triggered by the rapid appreciation of the yen, the trough could have been shallower, and the ensuing frenzy to stimulate the domestic demand and the resultant boom could have been moderated. The major deviation in the United States was at an early phase of the bubble in 2004, when tightening was less aggressive than the rule.

There was a difference in rhetoric: The Bank of Japan used lean-style languages and the Federal Reserve advocated a clean doctrine. It seems that, however, their behavior did not differ as much as the rhetoric suggests.

Also, the prudential policies in the two countries shared many common features.

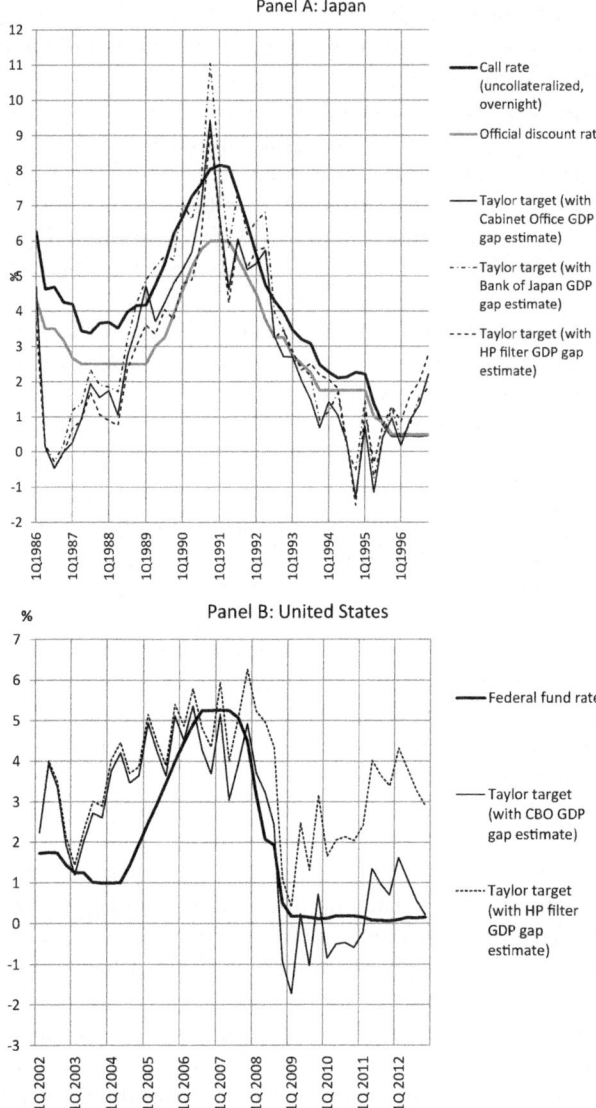

Fig. 3.3 Actual policy rates compared with Taylor targets (*Source* Himino 2016)

In the United States, as Table 3.2 shows, the federal regulators started to issue interagency guidelines in 1999, seven years before the residential real estate price peak and eight years before the commercial real estate price peak. They continued to add guidelines as the bubble grew, and after the residential real estate price peak in April 2006, implemented quantitative restrictions on commercial real estate-related lending (October 2006). A half year after the start of the restriction, the commercial real estate price peaked.

Regulators in Japan and the United States both started to introduce qualitative guidance very early in the boom, added layers of guidance as the bubble grew, and only after the initial signs of a bust, introduced quantitative limits, finishing off the boom and deepening the bust.

Table 3.2 Supervisory guidance issued by US authorities

March 1999	Interagency Guidance for Subprime Lending
October	Interagency Guidance on High Loan-to-Value (LTV) Residential Real Estate Lending
December	Interagency Guidance on Asset Securitization Activities
January 2001	Expanded Guidance for Subprime Lending Programs
February 2003	Interagency Advisory on Mortgage Banking
October	Interagency Guidance on Independent Appraisal and Evaluation Functions
April 2004	Interagency Guidance on Unfair or Deceptive Acts or Practices by State-Chartered Banks
February 2005	Interagency Guidance on the Detection, Investigation, and Deterrence of Mortgage Loan Fraud Involving Third Parties
March	Interagency FAQs on the Agencies' Appraisal Regulations and Interagency Statement on Independence of Appraisal and Evaluation Functions
May	Interagency Credit Risk Management Guidance for Home Equity Lending
May	Accounting and Reporting for Commitments to Originate and Sell Mortgage Loans
September	Interagency FAQs on Residential Tract Development Lending
October 2006	Interagency Guidance on Nontraditional Mortgage Product Risks
October	Addendum to the May 2005 Interagency Credit Risk Management Guidance for Home Equity Lending
December	<u>Interagency Guidance on Concentration in Commercial Real Estate Lending, Sound Risk Management Practices</u>
June 2007	Statement on Subprime Mortgage Lending

Note The underlined measure is quantitative, while others are qualitative
Source Cole (2007); Federal Reserve Board, Supervisory Policy and Guidance Topics: Real Estate (https://www.federalreserve.gov/supervisionreg/topics/real_estate.htm, accessed in November 2020)

In Hindsight

In hindsight, it seems that the monetary easing and major fiscal stimulus added in 1987, when the economy was recovering and the rapid land price hike started, may have been excessive. It may have been too late that monetary tightening started only in 1989. The QR should have been introduced earlier if it should have been introduced at all. The official discount rate was raised to 6% in 1990, when the stock price was plummeting and the six large city area land price peaked out. The QR was rescinded and the official discount rate was reduced only in the latter half of 1991. The combined effects of the monetary policy tightening and the QR may have been excessive in aggregate. In addition, perhaps the QR lasted too long.

The following four reasons may explain the delay in policy changes.

First, policy priorities other than moderating the boom and the bust prevented timely responses. The measures to contain bubbles were delayed as they were thought to conflict with the need to suppress the yen appreciation. The change in policy direction from containment of bubbles to the mitigation of their collapse was delayed as it was thought to go against the "crash the land myth" banner.

Policy choices have to be made under pressure from the public opinion and the political sector. Japan's experience shows that pressure can work in both directions, tightening and easing. Experts made better judgments in some cases, but in other, those who exerted pressure on experts seem to have had better insights. Policy authorities should try to engage constructively with the political sector and the public opinion, not taking the matter as a game of giving-in or not. If insights on the dynamics of bubbles and on the effects of policy measures could be shared widely in the society, constructive engagements would become easier.

Second, recognition lag may explain part of the delay. The land price indices during the period under study were published infrequently and with significant delays. Almost one year was needed to confirm the peak out of the land prices.[11] When it comes to making timely policy decisions, the Japanese authorities in the 1990s were far more disadvantaged than their US counterparts in the 2000s.[12] Today, more timely information is available in Japan than in the 1990s.[13]

The recognition lag is also significant regarding the peaks and troughs in business cycles. Seven months after the February 1991 peak, the government's monthly economic report modified its view from "in an expansion trend" to "still expanding with gradual deceleration" and after 11 months to "in an adjustment process." There are often several percentage points of difference between the first, second, and final estimates of the GDP growth rate. The final estimate is published nine to 18 months after the end of the estimated quarter. More frequent publication of more accurate economic statistics with smaller delay would help enable timely policy actions.

Prices of different asset classes peak out not simultaneously. The sequencing of the stock price peak and the real estate price peak was in reverse between Japan in the late 1980s and early 1990s and the United States in the 2000s. We cannot predetermine which index is a leading indicator. This makes the task of ascertaining a turning point even more difficult.

Third, the tax and land policy measures to reduce land prices were kept long after the collapse of the bubbles, perhaps because they had different objectives from those of macroeconomic or prudential policies.

For financial stability, the changes in land prices matter more than the level, but the levels matter more for taxation and redistribution purposes, since declining but high land prices still indicate land holders' capability to bear the tax burden. The levels matter more also for land policy, which aims to enable people to use land at reasonable prices.

Fourth, the Japanese authorities acted without the knowledge of what the bubbles and the crushes would cause later. This could have disadvantaged them.

But, even though the US authorities were well aware of what happened in Japan and were determined not to repeat its mistakes, the US monetary and prudential policies in the 2000s did not differ much from Japanese ones in the late 1980s and early 1990s. Knowing about others' mistake alone may not be enough to avoid repeating it ourselves.

NOTES

1. Nihon Keizai Shinbunsha (2000).
2. Nishimura (1999).
3. Kamikawa (2002).
4. For example, the Financial Services Agency in December 2006 added a footnote on the current conditions of the real estate market in its annual supervisory policy statement. The director general in charge published a related article in a business magazine. These gestures worked to contain the emerging real estate froth.

5. Karube (2015).
6. Nakai (2011).
7. Nishimura (1999).
8. For a lively and highly interesting description of the debate, see Chapter 6 of Friedman and Schwartz (1963).
9. Federal Reserve Bank of Kansas City (2003).
10. In Japan, the Nikkei 225 stock price index peaked in December 1989 and then six city area commercial land price index peaked in September 1990. In the United States, S&P Case-Shiller 10-City Home Price Index (Seasonally Adjusted) peaked in April 2006 and then the S&P 500 Stock Price Index peaked in October 2007.
11. The Urban Land Price Index by the Japan Real Estate Institute has been published semiannually and with a two-month lag. One could have noticed the start of a slight decline in six city area land price only eight months after the peak and could have confirmed a clear sign of decline only one year and two months after. If one used the Land Price Public Notice (January price with two month delay) and the Market Values of Standard Sites (July price with two month delay) both published by the National Land Agency, a similar recognition should have required four to six more months.
12. The Case-Shiller home price index and the Office of Federal Housing Enterprise Oversight home price index were published monthly with a two-month delay, and the First American Core Logic house price index monthly with a five week delay.
13. Available indices include: the Recruit Residential Price Index (monthly with one month delay), the Tokyo Stock Exchange Home Price Index (monthly with two month delay), the Japan Residential Property Price Index (monthly with four month delay) and the Trend Report of the Values of Intensively Used Land in Major Cities (quarterly).

REFERENCES

Ahearne, A. G., Gagnon, J., Haltmaier, J., Kamin, S. B., Erceg, C. J., Faust, J., & Wright, J. H. (2002). *Preventing deflation: Lessons from Japan's experience in the 1990s* (FRB International Finance Discussion Paper, No. 729).

Banking Bureau of the Ministry of Finance (Okurasho Ginko-kyoku). (1989). *The 38th annual report of the Banking Bureau (Dai 38 kai Ginkoukyoku Kin'yuu Nenpou)*. Kin'yuu Zaisei Jijou Kenkyuukai.

Banking Bureau of the Ministry of Finance (Okurasho Ginko-kyoku). (1991). *The 40th annual report of the Banking Bureau (Dai 40 kai Ginkoukyoku Kin'yuu Nenpou)*. Kin'yuu Zaisei Jijou Kenkyuukai.

Bernanke, B. S. (2002). On Milton Friedman's ninetieth birthday. In B. S. Bernanke (Ed.), *Remarks at the conference to honor Milton Friedman*. Chicago: University of Chicago.

Bernanke, B. S., & Gertler, M. (1999). Monetary policy and asset volatility. *Federal Reserve Bank of Kansas City Economic Review*. Fourth Quarter 1999, *84*(4), 17–52.

Borio, C., & White, W. R. (2003). Whither monetary and financial stability: the implications of evolving policy regimes. In *Proceedings-Economic Policy Symposium-Jackson Hole*. Federal Reserve Bank of Kansas City.

Cole, R. (2007, March 22). *Subprime mortgage market*. Testimony before the U.S. Senate Committee on Banking, Housing, and Urban Affairs.

Crowe, C., Dell'Ariccia, G., Igan, D., & Rabanal, P. (2014). Policies for macrofinancial stability: Managing real estate booms and busts. In S. Claessens, A. Kose, L. Laeven, & F. Valencia (Eds.), *Financial crises: Causes, consequences, and policy responses* (pp. 365–396). International Monetary Fund.

Federal Reserve Bank of Kansas City. (2003). *Monetary Policy and Uncertainty: Adapting to a Changing Economy*. Kansas City.

Friedman, M., & Schwartz, A. J. (1963). *A monetary history of the United States, 1867–1960*. Princeton: Princeton University Press.

Galbraith, J. K. (1954). *The great crash 1929*. Boston: Houghton Mifflin.

Hamada, K., Kashyap, A., & Weinstein, D. (2011). Introduction. In K. Hamada, A. Kashyap, & D. Weinstein (Eds.), *Japan's bubble, deflation, and long-term stagnation*. Cambridge: The MIT Press.

Himino, R. (2016). Japanese responses to asset price bubbles: Comparison with the US. *Public Policy Review*, *12*(2), 253–290.

Kamikawa, R. (2002). The bubble economy and the Bank of Japan independence (Baburu keizai to nihon ginkou no dokuritsusei). In M. Muramatsu & M. Okuno (Eds.), *Studies on Heisei bubbles, book 1, formation (Heisei baburu no kenkyu, Jou, Keisei hen)*. Toyo-keizai.

Karube, K. (2015). *Examination of the policy failures in dealing with the bubbles (Kenshou baburu shissei)*. Iwanami.

Nihon Keizai Shinbunsha. (2000). *Reviewing the bubbles: Mistakes made without intent (Kensho baburu han'i naki ayamachi)*. Nikkei Bijinesujin Bunko.

Nishimura, Y. (1999). *Why did the financial regulators fail? (Kinyu gyosei no haiin)*. Bunshun Bunko.

Okina, K., Shirakawa, M., & Shiratsuka, S. (2001). The asset price bubble and monetary policy: Japan's experience in the late 1980s and the lessons. *Monetary and Economic Studies*, *19*(2), 395–450.

Sei Nakai, S. (2011). Mr. Sei Nakai, 2nd interview, part 2, oral history (Dai 2 bu ooraru hisutori 2 nakai sei shi). In S. Matsushima & H. Takenaka (Eds.), *Oral history, Book 3, records on the Japanese economy (Nihon keizai no kiroku,*

3, *Jidai shougen shu, Oraru hisutori*). Economic and Social Research Institute, Cabinet Office.

Shiller, R. J. (2005). *Irrational exuberance*. New York: Broadway Books.

Taylor, J. B. (1993). Discretion versus policy rules in practice. *Carnegie-Rochester Conference Series on Public Policy, 39*, 195–214.

Tanizawa, E. (1995). *Wisdom on Human Being (Ningen tsuu)*. Shincho-sha.

White, W. R. (2009). *Should monetary policy 'lean or clean'?* (Federal Reserve Bank of Dallas, Globalization and Monetary Policy Institute Working Paper No. 34).

Yoshikawa, H. (2002). Land bubbles—Causes and backgrounds (Tochi baburu—gen'in to jidai haikei), Chapter 9. In T. Muramatsu & M. Okuno (Eds.), *Studies on bubbles in Heisei-era, Book 1 (Heisei Baburu no Kenkyu Jou)*. Toyo-keizai.

Open Access This chapter is licensed under the terms of the Creative Commons Attribution-NonCommercial-NoDerivatives 4.0 International License (http://creativecommons.org/licenses/by-nc-nd/4.0/), which permits any noncommercial use, sharing, distribution and reproduction in any medium or format, as long as you give appropriate credit to the original author(s) and the source, provide a link to the Creative Commons license and indicate if you modified the licensed material. You do not have permission under this license to share adapted material derived from this chapter or parts of it.

The images or other third party material in this chapter are included in the chapter's Creative Commons license, unless indicated otherwise in a credit line to the material. If material is not included in the chapter's Creative Commons license and your intended use is not permitted by statutory regulation or exceeds the permitted use, you will need to obtain permission directly from the copyright holder.

CHAPTER 4

In-Between Years

Abstract The period between the collapse of real estate bubbles and a banking crisis is less than two years in most crisis episodes in other countries but lasted for seven years in Japan. This chapter reviews how and why the Japanese authorities chose in 1992 to resort to banks' multi-year profits to resolve bad loans rather than to clean them up immediately.

Keywords In-between years · Bad loans · Catch 22 · P&A · *Jusen* · Market gridlock

In the Japanese case, the period between the real estate price peak (September 1990[1]) and the outbreak of the systemic banking crisis (November 1997) lasted more than seven years.

This was exceptionally long. Table 4.1 shows the corresponding periods for ten systemic banking crises in advanced economies since 1990. In seven episodes, the crisis occurred in the year of the real estate price peak or in the next. In one episode, two years later and in another, three years. None is comparable to the seven in-between years seen in Japan.

Table 4.1 In-between years in major banking crisis episodes since 1990

Country	Outbreak of banking crisis (A)	Residential real estate price peak (B)	Commercial real estate price peak (C)	B − A	C − A	Four-year cumulative output loss as percent of the trend GDP
Finland	1991	1989		2		69.6
Norway	1991	1988		3		5.1
Sweden	1991	1991		0		32.9
Japan	1997	1991	1990	6	7	45.0
United Kingdom	2007	2007		0		25.3
United States	2007	2006	2007	1	0	30.0
Denmark	2008	2007	2008	1	0	35.0
Ireland	2008	2007		1		107.7
Netherlands	2008	2008		0		26.1
Spain	2008	2007		1		38.8

Note Banking crises in advanced economies since 1990 for which real estate price peak years can be identified
Source For the crisis years and the output losses, Laeven and Valencia (2018). For the real estate price peak years, Bank for International Settlements, Long-term series on nominal residential property prices, and Commercial property price statistics

Estimating the Size of the Problem

In 1991, although the stock price was about 40% below the peak and the land price in large cities had already started to decline, still many Japanese had not realized how devastating the consequences would be. The government declared in October that the current expansion had become the longest in the post-World War II history of Japan, not recognizing that the business cycle had already peaked in February.

The first symptoms of the problem were a series of scandals. It was revealed in April 1991 that persons affiliated with a *yakuza* organized crime group had taken over the management of a trading firm and built a deep relationship with the CEO of a major bank, and that billions of dollars of loan from the bank to the firm had been syphoned to *yakuza*. In June, it was revealed that major securities houses had guaranteed investment returns to their major clients and had illegally compensated for their losses. In July and in August, two separate but similar incidents were revealed where bankers had issued false deposit certificates amounting to a billion dollars, which had been used as collateral for borrowing money for speculative purposes.

The nation had the impression that, though bankers had previously been well respected and trusted, some of them had badly been contaminated during the period of frenzy.

By early 1992, bankers and regulators started to realize that the bad loans created by the bubbles and the ensuing bust could be fatal to the Japanese banking system. Some journalists in and out of Japan were also aware of this.

The regulator carefully and narrowly defined bad loans when publishing the amount of them. In April 1992, the Ministry of Finance disclosed that as of March 1992 the amount of loans in arrear held by 21 major banks amounted to seven to eight trillion yen in gross and two to three trillion yen net of the parts covered by collaterals or guarantees. Two to three trillion yen of potential losses looked benign: the 21 banks' annual profits amounted to 0.94 trillion yen, and they had unrealized gain of 17 trillion yen on securities held.

But the definition covered only a fraction of the problem. They did not include the problem loans held by non-bank lenders affiliated to banks. They did not include doubtful loans not in arrears, including whose interest payments were financed by the lending banks.

At the time, there were no solid statistics of the total size of the problem based on the results of individual loan quality reviews. Regulators had only several rough estimates, which were highly dependent on the assumptions used. Naturally, the estimates failed to incorporate the effects of the subsequent land price declines, but still the numbers were totally ominous. According to Nishino (2003), the Ministry and the Bank of Japan in 1992 both privately estimated the gross amount of non-performing loans in the banking system to be much higher, somewhere between 30 and 50 trillion yen (Table 4.2).[2] Similar amount was reported by the Financial Times in May.

Table 4.2 Non-performing loan amounts estimated in 1992

As of	Type of NPL	NPL held by	NPL amount (trillion yen)
Private estimates by the Bank of Japan in early 1992[a]		All banks and shinkin banks	29
		21 major banks	21
Estimates published by the Ministry of Finance in April[b]	March 1992	Gross, in arrears	21 major banks	7–8
		Net, in arrears		2–3
Estimates reported by the Financial Times on its May 16 issue[c]	Sept 1991	Gross, including doubtful loans not in arrears	All financial institutions	42–53
			21 major banks	26.4–35.4
Private estimates by the Bank of Japan in August[d]				More than 40
Private estimates by the Ministry of Finance in August[e]				50
Estimates published by the Ministry of Finance in October	Sept 1992	Gross, in arrears	21 major banks	12.3
		Net, in arrears		4

Note As to b, later in September, the Ministry disclosed that the exact number was 7.9927 trillion yen at a session of a parliamentary committee. As to c, according to the Financial Times, the estimates were quoted from a report circulating among bankers in Tokyo, which was said to be based on confidential Bank of Japan data

Source Nishino (2003) for a and e. Nishino (2003) and Teramura (2011) for d

CATCH 22

The 30–50 trillion yen was a formidable number, amounting to 6–10% of the annual GDP. But the situation was even worse than the number suggests. In finding ways to resolve the bad loans, bankers and regulators faced with at least four types of Catch 22 style accelerator mechanism.

First, to resolve the bad loans, banks need to foreclose the borrowers and sell collaterals, making the land price decline further. Lower land price, however, increases bad loans and reduces the value of real estate collaterals.

4 IN-BETWEEN YEARS   51

Second, bad loans were not the only source of vulnerability on the Japanese banks' balance sheet. Japanese banks had large cross-shareholding with their customers. According to the simulation by the Ministry of Finance in the summer of 1992, if the Nikkei stock index had broken the 12,000 yen line, some banks would be in negative net worth, and if it had fallen below 10,000 yen, large number of banks, even without recognizing losses on bad loans.[3] The Nikkei index, which reached 38,915 yen at the end of 1989, recorded 14,194 yen on August 19, 1992, drawing near the red line. Banking problem can push down stock prices, and lower stock prices can exacerbate banking problem.

The third one was much more complicated. Loans extended by non-bank lenders amounted almost to 100 trillion yen. Around 80% of the debts of those lenders were financed by banks. Among the non-bank lenders, the seven Specialized Housing Finance Companies (*Jusens*) were particularly aggressive in making commercial real estate loans. They extended loans amounting 13 trillion yen in total, and the majority of them went sour.

Each of the *Jusens* were sponsored and owned by multiple banks. On average, they borrowed 30% of their debts from sponsoring banks, another 30% from non-sponsoring banks, and the remaining 40% from agricultural cooperatives.

Sponsoring banks could have been better off by resorting to a bankruptcy procedure, but once one *Jusen* should fail, then non-sponsoring banks and agricultural cooperatives, feeling betrayed by sponsoring banks, would start to run on other *Jusens*. Run could potentially affect other non-bank lenders.

Relationship between *Jusens*, banks, and agricultural cooperatives were entangled like spaghetti and no bankers or regulators had enough information to disentangle it.

The combination of the three booster mechanisms meant that once resolution of bad loans was started, bad loans would increase, the value of collaterals would decline, and the latent gains on equities held by banks may disappear or turn into latent losses.

The total size of the banking sector's own capital was as small as 30 trillion yen. The resolution of bad loans would expose that the whole banking sector, not just a handful of reckless banks, was severely undercapitalized or may have even been in negative net worth. To quickly resolve bad loans and keep the banking system and the economy alive, tens of trillions of yen of public support would have been needed.

But the national government's budget for fiscal year 1992 was 56 trillion yen, excluding the government's own debt service expenditure. Devoting the whole budget for SMEs (0.2 trillion yen) would have been totally insufficient. Even the whole social security budget (13 trillion yen) could have been dwarfed.

Here comes the fourth and the most important dilemma. The regulators needed public support for new resolution powers and an enormous amount of funding to avoid a systemic crisis. The series of bankers' scandals revealed in 1991 were surely not helpful in securing such support. Most likely, such political support can be acquired only after a systemic crisis. Of course regulators could have tried to convince the public that the amount of money was truly needed to avoid a catastrophe, but depositors' confidence in the banking system would then be lost half way through the persuasion and a catastrophe would be triggered before the law and budget were passed.

This kind of self-fulfilling prophecy was not without a precedent in the country. In 1927, the government submitted a bill to resolve banks' accumulated bad loans. The Diet deliberations revealed how bad the balance sheets of major banks were and the revelation caused the first wave of bank run before the bill was approved. Then a deterioration of the condition of one major bank resulted in the second wave of run, and the government tried to resort to an emergency imperial decree to bailout the bank. The public opinion got agitated, and the Privy Council rejected the proposal. The third and by far more devastating nationwide bank run ensued, and the government had to declare a three-week moratorium. Then an emergency session of the Diet approved a bailout bill in five days.[4] In 1992, the Ministry of Finance studied this episode, known as the Showa Financial Crisis, in depth and considered it as a guide to the crisis it was facing.

The Finance Ministry's Choice

The Ministry of Finance decided not to repeat the Showa Financial Crisis and to take necessary time to resolve bad loans. It hoped that banks' annual profits over years and unrealized capital gains on securities held by banks would eventually prove to suffice for the resolution of bad loans. The Ministry planned to request strong resolution tools and enough budgets only if the scenario should turn wrong and depositors should realize that their deposits were at risk.

An editorial which appeared on the Nikkei newspaper on May 29, 1992 describes a supervisory practice at the time: "Every year in April or in May, meetings are informally held at the Banking Bureau of the Ministry of Finance to give bankers administrative guidance how banks should account and publish the financial results for the accounting year ended in March. We see a few bankers sit in front of the desk of the Director,[5] and the conversation there *de facto* determines how the bank will report its annual financial results."

The editorial goes on to read between the lines of the financial reports published by major banks in May: "One can guess what was written in the clinical chart the Ministry prepared. The patients, ailing from the aftermath of the exuberance during the bubble economy, would not survive surgeries needed to cut off the diseased organs. The only available option is non-surgical, internal therapy of taking nutrition and waiting bad blood to be gradually purified. Or more explicitly, it must be that the Ministry instructed bankers not to throw away the affiliated non-bank lenders in trouble, but to support them with forbearance in interest rate and repayment schedules and with additional lending, and to make up the costs by annual income flows."

A high official in charge of banking supervision at the Ministry made the following remark to me during a private conversation in early 1992: "What I tell bankers these days is just this. Don't panic. Be patient."

The prescription which was implicit in banks' financial reports was made public in August 1992. The Ministry of Finance released a statement titled "Financial sector policies for the coming period." In its preamble, the Ministry stated:

> Banks are currently in a difficult condition they have never experienced since the start of the country's rapid economic growth after the World War II. . . . We cannot deny that, to overcome the impacts of the crash on banks, we need to continue rigorous and serious adjustment efforts for a significant period of time. . . . However, it is our firm belief that it is not inevitable that the problems will make the financial system dysfunction and put undue burden on the national economy. The problems can be overcome by avoiding simple pessimism and calmly laying many layers of steady and serious endeavors. . . .

Following the preamble, the statement laid out policy measures to prevent banks from beefing up their profits by realizing latent gains, to make banks come up with credible plans to deal with their non-bank affiliates, to create a market for liquidated collateral real estates, to enhance disclosure by banks, and to encourage banks to streamline their operations.

Many commentators argue that the policy statement showed that the Ministry was complacent and overlooked the seriousness of the problem. Perhaps these commentators overlooked the pathetic overtone of the statement and why the Ministry had to make repeated calls to be calm and steady.

The Bank of Japan and the Prime Minister

There were three attempts to challenge this line of thought, twice by the Bank of Japan and once by the prime minister.

The first attempt was made by the Bank of Japan. In May 1990, the Bank established a department responsible for financial stability. Upon the instruction by Governor Mieno to prepare for future bank failures, the head and the number three of the department visited authorities in the United States and Europe to learn from their experience.

In January 1991, the Bank's cross-department team reached a conclusion. An insolvent bank should be resolved, not by liquidation but by purchase and assumption approach (P&A),[6] as is the case with most failed banks in the United States. The Japanese Deposit Insurance Law, after its amendments in 1986, had indeed been equipped with the approach. Depositors should be protected, but the bank's management should be replaced, and shareholders should bear losses. If needed, the Deposit Insurance Corporation should provide financial assistance to support purchase and assumption operation, and the Bank of Japan should lend necessary amount of money.[7]

But the Ministry of Finance was not supportive of the principle that an insolvent bank should be resolved.[8] If the land price and the stock price should recover, banks with negative net worth would become solvent again. Why should we resolve them now, shock the nation, and prevent possible future recovery of asset prices? And if the asset prices should continue to deteriorate, then the whole banking sector would become insolvent. Can the recommended purchase and assumption approach resolve the whole banking system?

The second attempt was by the Prime Minister Miyazawa Kiichi himself. He was particularly worried about the stock price plunge in

August 1992 and even considered closing the Tokyo Stock Exchange. He was in frequent conversation with Governor Mieno of the Bank of Japan. According to Mieno (2007), he said to Miyazawa "It is already time to inject public funds, but the Ministry of Finance bureaucracy will never propose that to you. You yourself therefore need to instruct," and Miyazawa responded to him, "Well, is that so? I see, perhaps there is no other way than doing it myself." Mieno considered that Miyazawa saw what Mieno meant.

Miyazawa spoke at a seminar for ruling party members held at the end of August 1992:

> The growth rate of money supply declined from annual 10 percent to almost zero. Some argue that this is due to weak corporate financing needs, but the truth is the capacity of banks to lend is impaired by bad loans and other factors. The weak stock market reflects this. This is a factor unique to the current recession, which we have not experienced before.
>
> It is the responsibility of the government and the central bank to take necessary measures if the market economy ceases to function properly.
>
> We should create a mechanism to liquidate real estate collaterals held by banks by the end of the year as an element of the forthcoming economic policy package. The most desirable outcome is that financial institutions work together contributing their ideas and funds, but, if needed, I would not shy away from public support.
>
> This is not to save banks. Everyone would suffer if the blood ceases to circulate round the body of the national economy. I would not hesitate from doing what is needed for the whole national economy, on the condition that bankers behave in line with their public mission and disclose the amount of bad loans. The government and the central bank will never idly overlook future risk of financial instability.[9]

These were remarks given by the man of highest political power in the country, whose party had just won the upper house election the month before. But they were immediately reacted by criticism. Vice minister of finance, or the head of the civil service at the Ministry, denied in public any use of public money. Business leaders categorically rejected public support to banks. The chairman of the Bankers' Association stated that they will help themselves. Miyazawa abandoned the idea.

Later, in 1998–2001, Miyazawa served as finance minister. At the peak of the banking crisis, a congressman referred to his speech and asked him whether the crisis could have been alleviated if he, as the prime minister, had had the courage to resolve bad loans as proposed in his speech. Miyazawa responded, "I failed to enlist public opinion in support of my proposal. You asked me what if I had implemented the proposal, but I believe this is a clear case showing that any major surgery cannot be carried out without a support of the public opinion."[10]

The Ministry of Finance chose to wait till the condition was ripe. The prime minister demonstrated that the condition was not ripe and perhaps fortified the public allergy against the use of public funds by a premature proposal abruptly made without necessary political groundwork or a plan on the steps to be taken to reach the goal.

But the Bank of Japan did not give up. It made the third attempt: The Bank, after a deliberation at its policy board, submitted in May 1993 a report to the Ministry of Finance as a formal Bank of Japan proposal. The report assumed the amount of bad loans to be between 30 and 50 trillion yen. It included a detailed analysis of the banking problems and proposals for bank resolution and use of public funds, operationalizing the principles it proposed in 1991. However, the conversation between those who focused on what needs to be done and those who focused on what can be done was not easy.

If the Bank of Japan line of thought had prevailed, the four Catch 22 accelerator mechanisms would have been promptly activated, and perhaps Japan would have had a systemic banking crisis in 1992 or 1993. The period between the commercial real estate price peak in 1990 and the crisis would then have been two to three years, in line with the other crisis cases shown in Table 4.1. Which would have been better for the nation, a slow crisis which happened or a fast crisis which did not materialize?

After reviewing the whole developments of the financial cycle, we will come back to this question in Chapter 6.

Orderly Resolution Without Bailout[11]

The Ministry's strategy survived five more years. Strong balance-of-payment and net-external-asset positions of the country, trust in banks and the regulator built over decades of no bank failure, and accounting standards highly restrictive in provisioning against credit losses must have worked to sustain the strategy. But the strategy would not have survived without the concerted efforts by relevant players to attain orderly resolution overcoming the limitations in the toolbox.

In early 1994, the Ministry confirmed its view that latent gain on shares held by banks and annual profits would suffice to finance costs needed to resolve bad loans if enough time was given (Ministry of Finance 1994). But bad loans grew as land prices continued to decline, and it became evident that at least smaller and weaker links in the system could not survive. In 1995, the Ministry moved somewhat closer to the 1992 Bank of Japan view: It publicly confirmed that the total amount of bad loans in the system was around 40 trillion yen, that there could be cases that banks' own efforts might not suffice, and that issues including public involvement in resolution would need to be discussed (Ministry of Finance 1995).

The Japanese deposit insurance system started in 1971 with the only available option to pay out deposits with limited coverage. The purchase and assumption approach (P&A) was added in 1986, but the amount of financial assistance was capped at the payout cost, and the Ministry of Finance had to persuade other banks and local governments to contribute to fill the gap. During the in-between years, the Ministry faced the need to resolve 29 deposit taking institutions (banks, *shinkin* banks,[12] and credit cooperatives), but each case required joint tightrope acts by the Ministry, the Bank of Japan, the Deposit Insurance Corporation, and other stakeholders.

Initially, the Ministry succeeded in persuading existing bank to acquire failed banks, but the persuasion had become more and more difficult. Starting from 1994, some cases were resolved by establishing new recipient banks. In 1996, the national Diet passed the bill proposed by the Ministry to lift the limit on financial assistance by the Deposit Insurance Corporation on purchase and assumption. The deposit insurance fee was raised by seven times to finance the costs. It was also made possible for the Deposit Insurance Cooperation to borrow with government guarantee, but this option was allowed only to finance costs to resolve credit cooperatives, or the smallest members in the system.

This was the maximum the Ministry could attain before the outbreak of the systemic crisis. In 1996, the Ministry proposed to use 0.7 trillion yen of taxpayers' money to resolve seven *Jusens* . The money was needed to avoid incurring losses to politically mighty agricultural cooperatives, which lent to *Jusens*. The proposal was approved by the Diet, but the use of taxpayers' money to resolve reckless non-bank lenders attracted strong social anger.

To stabilize the banking system, much bigger amount of money was needed, but the public anger on 0.7 trillion yen made any further proposal on the use of public money politically untenable. To protect confidence in the system, preventive tools for banks which were distressed but not failed were indispensable, but the tools available at the time could be used only for the resolution of failed banks. The *Jusen* incident made it difficult to expand tools.

In November 1997, a medium-sized broker-dealer Sanyo Securities collapsed. Nobody thought it posed a systemic risk—it took no deposits and its operations were simple. However, its collapse resulted in the first default in the history of the Japanese interbank market. Although the size (about $10 million) was almost negligible, a few days later the interbank money market started to freeze up. In a stressed environment, a seemingly non-systemic case can have a systemic signaling effect and trigger a chain reaction.

Ten days later, Hokkaido Takushoku Bank, one of the countrys leading 20 banks, and Yamaichi Securities, one of the top four broker-dealers, both encountered with liquidity shortage. The Ministry of Finance, with the help of the Bank of Japan, found a recipient bank for the former over the weekend and the purchase and assumption was announced in the afternoon of Sunday, November 16.

There was no resolution framework for broker-dealers. Given that Yamaichi had a big derivatives book and significant cross-border exposures, the Bank of Japan decided to provide uncollateralized liquidity support. On November 24, Yamaichi announced that it will wind itself down.

The Ministry of Finance, the Bank of Japan, and the Deposit Insurance Corporation, all very thinly staffed, overcome enormous obstacles despite extremely tight schedule and successfully orchestrated orderly resolutions. No depositors or creditors suffered loss except for creditors to Sanyo Securities. Nevertheless, the succession of big-name resolutions shocked the nation. In addition, the Deposit Insurance Corporation had already run out of its policy reserve by March 1997 and the size of financial assistance needed to achieve the purchase and assumption transaction for the Hokkaido Takushoku Bank, four times as large as the annual premium, was far beyond its financial resources.[13]

On November 25, due to an unfounded rumor, queues were formed at branches of one regional bank. Early in the morning of November 26, the resolution of another regional bank through purchase and assumption was announced.

The day November 26, 1997, started with dark clouds hanging over the archipelago. The in-between years were coming to an end.

Notes

1. As the Japanese banking crisis was primarily triggered by commercial real estate bubbles rather than residential real estate ones, the commercial real estate price peak date is used in measuring the Japanese interval period.
2. Teramura (2011), who was the director general of the Banking Bureau of the Ministry of Finance at the time, confirms the report by Nishino (2003) that the Bank of Japan informed its estimate of above 40 trillion yen to the Ministry in August 1992. According to Teramura (2011), the Ministry made an own estimate amounting to 42 trillion yen in early 1994.
3. Teramura (2010).
4. See Takahashi and Morigaki (1993).
5. At Japanese government ministries, the whole members of a division usually work in a single room. At the time, bankers and accredited reporters could freely enter Finance Ministry offices.
6. Purchase and assumption approach is a resolution method in which another bank purchases failed bank's assets and assumes its obligations with financial assistance provided by the resolution authority. In the first two cases of its application in Japan, failed banks' whole assets were purchased by sound banks, but starting from the third case, sound banks purchased only sound assets and bad loans were transferred to third parties.
7. Shirakawa (2018).
8. Ibid.
9. August 31, 1992 morning editions of Asahi, Nikkei, and Mainichi (newspapers), and Iokibe et al. (2006).
10. Response by Finance Minister Miyazawa Kiichi to the question by Councilor Sato Michio at the Special Committee on Financial Issues and Revitalization of the Economy at the 143rd session of the House of Councilors (Upper House) on October 7, 2018.
11. For bank failures and the evolution of the resolution approaches during the in-between years, see Nakaso (2001) and Deposit Insurance Corporation of Japan (2007).

12. Both *shinkin* banks and credit cooperatives are non-profit mutual organizations which do banking business with individuals and SMEs in their region of operation. Larger SMEs are eligible to become members of *Shinkin* banks but not credit cooperatives.
13. The deposit insurance premium rate was raised in the fiscal year 1996 to the level seven times as high as the previous level, but the annual premium received after the raise was about 0.46 trillion yen, while assistance to the recipient bank of the Hokkaido Takushoku amounted to 1.8 trillion yen.

REFERENCES

Deposit Insurance Corporation of Japan (Yokin Hoken Kikou). (2007). *Responses to the financial crisis in the Heisei era—How did the deposit insurance function? (Heisei kin'yuu kiki eno taiou – Yokin hoken wa ikani kinou shitaka)*. Kin'yuu Zaisei Jijou Kenkyuukai.
Iokibe, M., Ito, M., & Yakushiji, K. (2006). *Testimony on the 1990s: Miyazawa Kiichi, The trajectory of a Main-stream Conservative (90-nendai no Shougen: Miyazawa Kiichi. Hoshu Honryu no Kiseki)*. Asahi Shimbun Sha.
Laeven, L., & Valencia, F. (2018). *Systemic banking crises revisited* (IMF Working Paper WP/18/206).
Mieno, Y. (2007). *Record of oral history by Former Governor Mieno Yasushi (Mieno Yasushi Moto-Sousai no Ooraru Hisutorii ni tsuite)*. Institute of Monetary and Economic Studies, Bank of Japan.
Ministry of Finance. (1994). *Administrative guidelines on financial institutions' bad loan problems (Kin'yuu kikan no furyou saiken mondai ni tsuiteno gyouseijou no shishin)*.
Ministry of Finance. (1995). *On restoring the function of the financial system (Kin'yuu shisutemu no kinou kaifuku ni tsuite)*.
Nakaso, H. (2001). *The financial crisis in Japan during the 1990s: How the Bank of Japan responded and the lessons learnt* (BIS Papers No. 6).
Nishino, T. (2003). *Keizai An'un (Dark clouds covering the economy)*. Iwanami.
Shirakawa, M. (2018). *Central Bank: 39 years of a central banker (Chuuou Ginkou: Sentoral Bankaa no Keiken shita 39 nen)*. Toyo Keizai.
Takahashi, K., & Morigaki, S. (1993). *The history of the showa-era financial crisis (Shouwa Kin'yuu Kyoukou Shi)*. Koudansha Gakujutsu Bunko.
Teramura, N. (2010). Resolving non-banks during continued decline in stock and land prices (Kabuka fudousan gerakuka deno nonbanku shori). In Kin'yuu Zaisei Jijou, *The trajectory of struggle by financial sector policy aiming deregulation (Jiyuuka Gyousei Kutou no Kiseki)*.
Teramura, N. (2011). Mr. Nobuyuki Teramura (Teramura Nobuyuki shi). In S. Matsushima & H. Takenaka (Eds.), *Testimony of the time; oral history,*

records on the Japanese economy *(Nihon keizai no Kiroku, Jidai shougen shuu; Ooraru Hisutorii)*. Economic and Social Research Institute, Cabinet Office (Naikakufu Keizai Shakai Sougou Kenkyuujo).

Open Access This chapter is licensed under the terms of the Creative Commons Attribution-NonCommercial-NoDerivatives 4.0 International License (http://creativecommons.org/licenses/by-nc-nd/4.0/), which permits any noncommercial use, sharing, distribution and reproduction in any medium or format, as long as you give appropriate credit to the original author(s) and the source, provide a link to the Creative Commons license and indicate if you modified the licensed material. You do not have permission under this license to share adapted material derived from this chapter or parts of it.

The images or other third party material in this chapter are included in the chapter's Creative Commons license, unless indicated otherwise in a credit line to the material. If material is not included in the chapter's Creative Commons license and your intended use is not permitted by statutory regulation or exceeds the permitted use, you will need to obtain permission directly from the copyright holder.

CHAPTER 5

Crisis

Abstract The seven in-between years ended with a banking crisis, which brought Japan to the brink of a systemic meltdown. The crisis was contained with massive capital injections in banks, much-enhanced resolution tools, stronger disclosure and provisioning, and the new supervisory agency. The crisis, however, resulted in credit crunch, recession, bankruptcy, unemployment, and suicide and left deep scars in the Japanese economy and society.

Keywords Bank run · Resolution tools · Disclosure · Provisioning · Supervisory culture · Credit crunch

At around ten in the morning on Wednesday November 26, 1997, telephones at the headquarters of the Bank of Japan and the Ministry of Finance started to ring with emergency reports from their local offices, and from bankers.[1] Queues of depositors were formed in front of bank branches in Wakayama, Utsunomiya, Toyama, Sapporo, Tokyo, Nagoya, Osaka, and Fukuoka. Bank equity prices started to tumble, and the short-term money market rate jumped up.

The anxiety accumulated in the minds of the nation through the series of bank failures was reaching a critical level. According to Nakaso (2001), who then was the director in charge of financial stability at the Bank of Japan, "This was probably the day that Japan's financial system was closest to a systemic collapse." Later, a Finance Ministry high official recalled the day and said, "We peeped into the boiling pot of the Hell."[2]

The Ministry instructed banks to contain the queues by giving depositors numbered cards and guide them to meeting rooms inside branches, lest the scene of a queue should lure other depositors to join the run. The Bank of Japan dispatched enormous amount of cash, since depositors would panic if a branch should run out of cash. In the evening of the day, the minister of finance and the governor of the Bank of Japan issued a joint statement confirming that deposits and interbank exposures would be protected. The heads of the local branches of the Ministry and the Bank in the affected regions held joint press conferences to calm the depositors. Banks showed video-taped press conferences at branches.

TV stations refrained from broadcasting the queues and newspapers refrained to report. There were no social networking services or internet banking in those days. The queues subsided in the following days. But many did not believe that it was the end of the horror. A psychiatrist Nakai Hisao describes his feeling in mid-December as follows: "I felt like a passenger on a ship, who found that a torpedo was heading straight towards the ship. Knowing that there was no way to avert it, I held the handrail tight and waited for the moment of impact."[3]

Political Leadership

Political leaders sensed the nation's inquietude earlier than the day of the nationwide queues. Four days after the collapse of the Hokkaido Takushoku Bank, former prime minister Miyazawa submitted to the prime minister a proposal to use public funds. On the next day, another ruling party heavyweight Kajiyama Seiroku also submitted a proposal. The day after the collapse of the Yamaichi Securities and the day before the queue day, the ruling Liberal Democratic Party established the Emergency Headquarters for Financial Stability and nominated Miyazawa as its head.

Miyazawa proposed to use public funds to assist resolution of failed banks by supporting purchasing banks. Kajiyama proposed preemptive capital injection to banks which have not yet failed. In Miyazawa's proposal, the government was to guarantee bonds issued by the Deposit

Insurance Corporation, and, in Kajiyama's, to grant funds to the Corporation. Miyazawa did not mention a specific amount of money, and Kajiyama, ten trillion yen.

The ruling party proposal agreed in December was beefed up to more than the sum of the two proposals. The government will guarantee the borrowing by the Deposit Insurance Corporation and provides funds to it.[4] The money can be used both for assisting purchasers of failed banks and for supporting living banks. The amount of money was increased to thirty trillion yen.

A Finance Ministry high official later recounted, "While deliberating on the proposal, the ruling party started to realize that the public opinion was now not so hostile to the use of public funds. Then the party turned passionate about the project and started to think that, if they should do it, they should do it big. Politicians are good at grasping emerging opportunities. I believe the bureaucracy is for continuity and the politics is for a jump."

Nakai Sei, who struggled to sustain the system at the Ministry during the in-between years, argues, "The nation could accept the use of public funds only after a financial crisis became a reality and the economy was brought to the brink of a panic."[5]

Capital Injections and Raids on Regulators

The Finance Ministry officials worked day and night and, in January 1998, submitted to the national Diet bills implementing the ruling parties' recommendations.

The Diet passed the two new laws on 16 February. The Japanese banks' accounting year ends at the end of March. Just in time for this deadline, the 1.8 trillion-yen assistance to the banks purchasing the Hokkaido Takushoku Bank was financed based on one of the two laws. Preemptive capital injections were made to 21 banks based on the other law. The amount of injected capital, 1.8 trillion yen, was totally inadequate to resurrect 21 banks, most of them much larger than Hokkaido Takushoku, but the injection demonstrated that the government stood ready to support them. A crisis, which had been feared to happen at the end of March, was averted by a hairsbreadth.

According to Nishino (2019), when the ruling party started to discuss the use of public funds, officials at the Banking Bureau of the Ministry of Finance was wary, thinking "If the use of public funds gets discussed, then we will be hanged, drawn, and quartered."

The prediction was not too much off the mark. One day after the submission of the bills to the Diet, the coalition ruling parties formally agreed to break up the Ministry of Finance into the fiscal policy part and the financial supervision part sometime in 1998. The decision concluded the deliberations lasted for two years since February 1996, when the use of public funds to resolve *Jusens* ignited the review on the Ministry.

Amid the Diet deliberations, the Tokyo Prosecutors' Office raided the Ministry headquarters. The Ministry's two bank inspectors were arrested on the charges of having been entertained by banks. The minister and the vice minister resigned, and one senior inspector committed suicide.

While a newly created panel examined major banks' applications for capital injections, other two Finance Ministry officers and a Bank of Japan director were arrested, the Ministry's another officer committed suicide, the Prosecutors' Office raided the Bank of Japan headquarters, and the governor and the deputy governor of the Bank resigned.

One month after the capital injection, the Ministry fired the director general of the Securities Bureau and the deputy director general of the Banking Bureau and imposed disciplinary measures on other 110 officers for being entertained by financial institutions. The Bank of Japan took measures on 98 officers.

SUMMER 1998

In 1998, the rainy season started earlier than usual. A rainy season usually lasts for one month and a half, but in that year, it continued to rain throughout the summer. In some parts of Japan, it was difficult to identify when the season ended.

On Friday June 5, 1998, a Japanese monthly magazine carried an article with an eerie title "The failure of the Long-Term Credit Bank of Japan (LTCB) will trigger a terrifying process to weed out weak banks." On the following Monday, the Financial Times reported on problems at the LTCB. On Tuesday, the London branch of the joint venture investment bank formed by the LTCB and a foreign bank sold 1.4 million LTCB shares. Market participants thought that the foreign bank, which agreed on an alliance with the LTCB about a year ago, was now turning its back to its partner.

The LTCB share price tumbled to less than a quarter of the price seen in May. Run on the bank ensued both in branches in Japan and in money market in London. The foreign alliance partner gained the right to acquire the full ownership of three joint venture firms based on the "distress warrant clause" added to the joint venture agreements three month before, which used the LTCB share price as the trigger.

The LTCB was established in 1952 under the newly enacted Long-Term Credit Bank Act. It had the privilege to issue debentures, which was given to only a handful of banks, and financed investments in factories and equipment. It substituted Japan's immature capital market and supported the country's rapid economic growth in the 1960s. But by the mid-1980s, the Japanese manufacturers stopped building factories in Japan, and large companies started to finance themselves in the overseas capital market. The bank's unique *raison d'être* largely disappeared.

The bank considered several options. One was to downsize and transform itself to a boutique investment bank, building on its strength in the capital market and cross-border transactions. Another was to expand itself to be like other ordinary commercial banks. The bank tried to pursue both options, but the former was frustrated by the Japanese version of Glass-Steagall. The latter faced the lack of a large branch network needed to lend to SMEs and an affiliated *keiretsu* group needed to lend to big businesses.

Toward the end of the asset price bubbles, the LTCB and its affiliated non-bank lenders found opportunities for growth and profit in loans to emerging real estate developers. Its balance sheet swelled to the size equivalent to that of Citicorp or Société Générale, making it the world's 20th largest. After the collapse of the real estate price bubble, swelled loans went sour.

According to Suzuki (2009), who served as the bank's last CEO, the LTCB first focused on the resolution of bad loans extended by the bank itself, and then from 1994 expanded the scope of its efforts to the restructuring of its affiliated non-bank lenders. The eight years of struggle with bad loans were like "trying to climb up vertical cliffs of a rocky mountain one after another." He refers to the involvement of *yakuza* organized crimes which supported borrowers and obstructed the bank, very illiquid real estate market and lack of secondary markets for loans, slow and cumbersome legal process needed to auction collateral real estates, and other difficulties. The LTCB bankers, who had lent only to the cream of the Corporate Japan for decades, had to deal with totally different types of people.

The series of events in June 1998 happened at the most inconvenient period for both the government bureaucracy and for the political leadership to fulfil their crisis management roles. In the month, the Ministry of Finance was teared apart. Regulatory policy stayed with the Ministry and supervisory power was vested in the newly created Financial Supervisory Agency (JFSA). The new Agency was just organizing itself and was in short even of stationary, not to speak of experienced staff. There were some doubts on which of the two, the Ministry or the Agency, should take the lead in managing the crisis.

In July, the ruling Liberal Democratic Party lost heavily at the Upper House election. The Party president cum the prime minister resigned, and the party's new presidency was contested between Kajiyama Seiroku, who argued for a "hard-landing" policy of resolving bad loans in two years, and Obuchi Keizo, who argued for what could be called a "soft-landing" policy of supporting the economy by fiscal stimulus and won the contest. Having lost the majority at the Upper House, the ruling party could not enact a law without supports by oppositions.

Deciding on the resolution of an internationally active big bank under the condition of a system-wide distress cannot be an easy task anyway, but in this case the process coincided with the distress in the government. The LTCB had been put in limbo for more than four months.

During the four months, the debate continued both on the design of the country's resolution framework in general and on the fate of the LTCB in particular.

On the resolution framework, the ruling party was for the use of a bridge bank, and the opposition parties were for introducing a temporary nationalization approach. On October 12, the Diet enacted a bill to introduce both the bridge bank approach and the temporary nationalization approach. In addition, on October 16, the Diet enacted a bill to earmark 25 trillion yen for preemptive capital injections, 18 trillion yen for resolving failed banks, and 17 trillion yen for depositor protection, doubling the available amount of public funds to 60 trillion yen, or 11% of the annual GDP.

On the LTCB, there were debates involving the ruling party, the opposition parties, the Ministry of Finance, and the Financial Supervisory Agency. Some were leaning toward persuading a sounder bank to rescue the LTCB, while others were for resolving it as a failed bank.

The bank's fate took the latter course, as a candidate rescuing bank refused to step in, even though the prime minister and the finance minister themselves tried to persuade it in person. On October 23, the LTCB was nationalized as a failed bank. Later, the bank was assessed to be of negative net worth amounting to 2.7 trillion yen, or 11% of its total asset. In December, the Nippon Credit Bank, another of the three long-term credit banks, was nationalized.

In December, the Financial Reconstruction Commission was established to administer bank resolution and capital injection. In January 1999, the Commission announced that banks should provision at least for around 15% of the outstanding uncollateralized amount of substandard loans and 70% of doubtful loans. By the end of March, major banks had 7.5 trillion yen of capital injected by the Commission and raised 2.6 trillion yen in the market. The crisis started in November 1997 largely subsided in March 1999.

But the immediate remedial measures to contain symptoms can stay credible only when accompanied by longer-term policies that address the diseases and deeper causes. A crisis can provide a rare opportunity for painful but needed reforms. Many important steps had been taken by March 1999 as described below, but more had to be done, as will be described in Chapter 6.

Evolution of Resolution Approaches

During the crisis period from November 1997 to March 1999, Japan gained and lost many things. Among the most important gains was a much-enhanced toolkit for resolution (Table 5.1).

The resolution approaches, which initially covered only failed banks, were expanded to cover failing banks and distressed banks in 1998. The coverage of protection was expanded from insured deposits to all liabilities in 1996. Approaches which can maintain the legal entity was introduced in 1998 to limit disruptions in derivatives, lending, and other markets. The previous set of tools had been able to deal only with idiosyncratic failures of non-systemic banks, but the toolkit was now capable of addressing system-wide distress and resolving internationally active systemic banks.

Table 5.1 Evolution of resolution approaches

Approaches	Liquidation without deposit insurance	Liquidation with deposit insurance	P&A with financial assistance	Temporary nationalization	Preemptive capital injection
Introduced in	–	1971	Limited assistance 1986, Unlimited assistance 1996	October 1998	February 1998
Banks to be resolved	Failed bank			Failed or failing bank	Distressed bank
Insured deposit	Not protected	Protected			
Uninsured debt	Not protected		Protected		
Equity	Invalidated				Diluted
Legal entity	Liquidated			Kept	
Management	Replaced by liquidator		Fired on transfer Replaced by financial administrator (1998-)	Replaced by new team	Recovery plan monitored
Use cases	BCCI Tokyo branch (1991) Sanyo Securities (1997)		177 banks, shinkin banks, and credit cooperatives (1991–2001) Incubator Bank of Japan (2010, with limited assistance)	LTCB (1998) NCB (1998) Ashikaga Bank (2003)	21 banks (1998) 15 banks (1999) 19 banks (1999–2003) including Resona Bank (2003)

Source Author's compilation

Disclosure, Provisioning, and Corrective Actions

With the new resolution approaches and funding arrangements provided, the Japanese authorities were freed from the Catch 22 type predicament and started to introduce framework to recognize and address problems without further forbearance. Disclosure and provisioning standards were enhanced, and the treatment of undercapitalized banks was anchored to numerical criteria.

If we are to use the metaphor used by the Nikkei *op-ed* piece in 1992 cited in Chapter 4, now that the operation theater was set up with a range of surgical tools and with enough blood for transfusion, doctors need not to hesitate making timely diagnosis or prescription.

First, the standards on bad loan disclosure were strengthened. The Financial Supervisory Agency aimed to align the Japanese disclosure standards with those established by the US Securities and Exchange Commission. Previously, only loans in arrears for more than six months and loans lent with interest rates below the official discount rates had been included in the definition of the non-performing loans. Now loans in arrears for more than three months and loans lent with interest rates below the market rates were included. The reported outstanding amount of bad loans of major banks at the end of March 1998 was 16 trillion yen under the previous standards and 22 trillion yen under the new standards. The disclosure on a consolidated basis was made a legal obligation with penalties for derogations. Common minimum disclosure items were specified, and their definitions were clarified by the authority.[6]

Second, loan loss provisioning was strengthened. The amount of annual loss resulting from bad loan provisioning, sales, and write off jumped from 8 trillion yen in fiscal year 1997 to 13 trillion yen in FY 1998, and 14 trillion yen in FY 1999. Previously, only the amount unrecoverable had to be written off, and provisioning on doubtful loans beyond the predetermined ratio (3%) was at banks' discretion. In 1998, provisioning for doubtful loans was made mandatory, and as mentioned above, the Financial Reconstruction Commission announced in January 1999 that banks should provision at least for around 15% of the outstanding uncollateralized amount of substandard loans and 70% of doubtful loans. Before, provisioning required regulators' prior approval, but, starting from fiscal year 1998, banks were mandated to make proper provisions and write-offs on their own responsibility. Regulators would not provide ex ante approval. They conduct ex post review only.

Third, a framework of prompt corrective action was introduced for internationally active banks from April 1998 and for other banks from April 1999. The framework prescribed regulatory action according to banks' capital adequacy ratio. A bank operating slightly below the minimum ratio will be required to submit a plan to augment its capital base, whereas a deeply undercapitalized bank may be ordered to terminate its baking business. The framework was initially proposed by the Ministry of Finance in 1995, and a relevant law was passed in 1996. The Ministry's effort provided the newborn Agency with a transparent framework for regulatory actions.

New Supervisory Culture

A new supervisory authority, the Financial Supervisory Agency (JFSA), was inaugurated in June 1998 amid the turmoil surrounding the LTCB. It started with totally insufficient resources but created a new supervisory culture.

The Agency was responsible for the supervision of banks, insurance companies, broker-dealers, and asset managers and the surveillance of the capital market of what then was the second largest economy in the world. If compared with US regulatory authorities, the Agency's scope of responsibility corresponded to that of the OCC, the supervision division of the FRB, part of FDIC, state bank and insurance regulators, SEC, and part of CFTC. But, despite being amid a crisis, it had only 403 staff members at its headquarters. In early days of the Agency, the deputy head of the Agency Hamanaka Hideichiro used to say, "If a staff member has got only two different assignments, he should be ashamed of not doing enough. Three may be acceptable, and four can qualify him as hard-working."

The Finance Ministry had very few professional lawyers, accountants, economists, or actuaries to begin with. Moreover, experienced regulators who had been entertained by banks could not been transferred to the new Agency. Some at the Agency's leadership positions had little previous experience of supervising financial institutions. Computers were slow, printers were scarce, and paper, pencils, and highlighter pens were in short supply. In the middle of the negotiations on Basel II, the overseas travelling budget was depleted.

More importantly, the new Agency was little known to the nation and was without any accumulated moral authority or reputation capital. Even on matters within the jurisdiction of the JFSA, many congressmen preferred to discuss with the Ministry of Finance rather than with the obscure new agency. A newspaper carried a cartoon depicting officers lined up on the deck of a big warship, who waved their hands at a small boat being hanged down from the warship to a turbulent sea.

But the inaugurate staff members, who later were dubbed as Pilgrim Fathers, were filled with frontier spirits. There was a clear break in the culture between the big warship and the small boat. The latter's culture was closer to a start-up venture than to a big organization with power and history.

On the day of the inauguration, the prime minister instructed Commissioner Hino Masaharu, the new head of the Agency, to focus on ex post reviews, not on ex ante administrative guidance. He demanded that the Agency's activities be fair and transparent, that staff members uphold high ethical standards and re-establish trusts on regulators, and that the Agency do utmost to facilitate resolution of bad loans held by financial institutions.

Responding to this request for a clean break from the previous banking supervision, Commissioner Hino, a former criminal prosecutor, pledged in his inaugural press conference to conduct fair and transparent supervision based on articulate and transparent rules and standards. The Agency shall conduct rigoros and effective on-site inspections and off-site monitoring and act on facts and evidence gathered.

On the day, the director general Gomi Hirofumi of the on-site inspection department instructed inspectors as follows:

> The nation doubts if you discharge your responsibility properly. The only thing you need to do now is to report back what you saw on the inspection sites without any distortions. You are radiographers and your responsibility is taking accurate X-rays. The diagnosis is the responsibility of doctors, not yours. Forget about any possible consequences of X-rays taken. Don't hesitate. Consolidate what you have seen and report facts.[7]

Gomi also argued that the Agency should disclose information to have it sanitized by airing and sunshine. The director general of the supervision department Inui Fumio had repeatedly mentioned the following three principles to himself and staff members: Never lie, never hide, and never postpone.

Shiga Sakura, who was the head of the international division, learned about a forbearance policy considered within the Agency while he was travelling abroad. Infuriated, he sent to Tokyo a facsimile message with handwritten big letters, stating, "Otto von Bismarck once said, 'Only a fool learns from his own mistakes. The wise man learns from the mistakes of others.' He would consider us worse than a fool." A copy of the message was posted on the wall of the international division for many years.

CREDIT CRUNCH, RECESSION, BANKRUPTCY, UNEMPLOYMENT, AND SUICIDE

At the same time, the crisis left deep scars in the Japanese economy and society. The crisis triggered a severe credit crunch, and it coincided with fiscal austerity and the Asian financial crisis. The combined effects resulted in recession and surges in bankruptcy, unemployment, and suicide.

The failures of major banks and the long queues of depositors around the country in November 1997 scared bankers. They were further intimidated by the scene of the world's 20th largest bank put in limbo for four month and by the new regulators' repeated declaration of the end of forbearance. Bankers rapidly tightened their lending standards, despite the repeated easing of the monetary policy during the period. The difference between the proportions of firms facing "easy" and "tight" bank lending attitude dropped from positive 14 percentage points in the third quarter of 1997 to negative 19 points in the first quarter of 1998.[8] While only 78 newspaper and magazine articles referred to "credit crunch" in 1996, the number jumped to 2330 in 1997 and then exploded to 15,869 in 1998.[9] The outstanding amount of bank loans to the non-financial corporate sector, which stayed flat during the in-between years, started to decline.

And the credit crunch coincided with fiscal austerity, on which the government embarked in January 1997. The VAT and income tax were raised in April 1997, and larger share of medical expenses were put on patients in September.

The business cycle had peaked in May. The Asian financial crisis broke out in July and the Japanese banking crisis in November. The fiscal policy had to make a rapid turnabout. The new fiscal consolidation law, enacted early in December, was de facto abandoned later in the month by the decision to cut the income tax.

The real growth rate declined from 3% in 1996 to 1% in 1997 and turned negative in 1998. Motonishi and Yoshikawa (1999) estimate that the credit crunch lowered the GDP growth rate by 1.6 percentage points. The government tried to mitigate the credit crunch by expanding the budgets for the public guarantee of loans to SMEs and for the direct lending by government financial institutions each by 20 trillion yen. It also published in November 1998 the largest economic stimulus package in the history. It was composed of tax cuts and infrastructure investments and amounted to 4% of the annual GDP. The government bond issuance almost doubled from 18.5 trillion yen in the fiscal year 1997 to 34.0 trillion yen in the fiscal year 1998.

The fiscal consolidation law was formally terminated on December 2, 1998, and Moody's Investor Service downgraded the Japanese Government Bond (JGB) on December 17. A newspaper article reported on December 20 that the government-run Fiscal Investment and Loan Program would reduce the purchase of JGBs. The 10-year JGB rate jumped from less than 0.8% in early October 1998 to 2.4% in early February 1999.

But contrary to what happened to the Eurozone in the 2010s, selling-off of the JGB did not lead to selling-off of Japan. The yen, which was traded at around 135 yen per dollar in early October 1998, rose by a quarter to 109 yen per dollar in early January 1999, exerting further deflationary pressure on the economy.

The Bank of Japan then entered the brave new world of the unconventional monetary policy. It introduced the world's first zero interest rate policy (ZIRP) in March 1999. In April it announced that it would continue ZIRP till the deflationary concern was dispelled, introducing the world's first forward guidance. The 10-year JGB rate declined to 1.3% in May and the yen depreciated to the level of 120 yen per dollar.

The fiscal stimulus, which doubled the deficit, and the unconventional monetary policy, which had been deployed a decade before the United States and Europe did, were successful in averting an acute deflationary spiral, and the business cycle bottomed in January 1999. Nevertheless, the growth rate in 1999 stayed negative.

The experience highlighted the need to coordinate various elements of economic policy. The Council on Economic and Fiscal Policy was inaugurated in 2001, with the prime minister as its chair and five ministers, the governor of the Bank of Japan, two business leaders, and two economists as its members, and strengthened its role over time.

The annual cases of corporate bankruptcy jumped from 15 thousand in 1996 to 19 thousand in 1998 (Fig. 5.1). The Economic Planning Agency (1999) argues that factors on the side of banks contributed to the increase in corporate bankruptcy cases, particularly in 1998. Although employers tried to maintain employment by reducing overtime, restraining pay, and sacrificing corporate profits, the unemployment rate hiked from 3.5% in end 1997 to 4.4% in end 1998 and 4.7% in end 1999, breaking the record.

In the post-war Japan, there was a system of implicit chain of support: the Ministry of Finance reigns over and looks after banks, banks monitor, support and, if necessary, intervene in big businesses, big businesses often take advantages of subcontractors but in certain cases protect them, and employers demand full dedication from their employees but in return guarantee lifetime employment. 1998 was the year when this social contract of the post-war Japan was shaken and cracked.

Up until 1997, the annual number of people committing suicide has long fluctuated between 20 thousand and 25 thousand. It, however, jumped to 33 thousand in 1998 and stayed around the level even after the unemployment returned to the pre-crisis level (Fig. 5.1). The crack in the system caused by the crisis was deeply unnerving and painful.

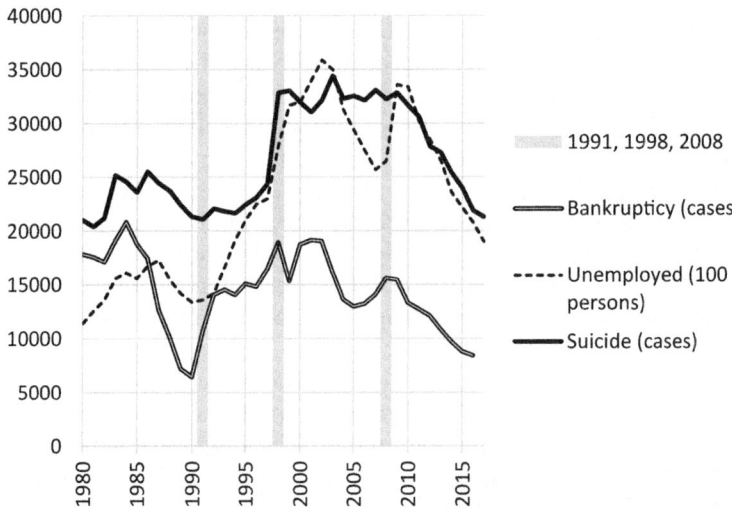

Fig. 5.1 Bankruptcy, unemployment, and suicides (*Source* Tokyo Shoko Research, National corporate bankruptcies; Statistics Bureau, Labor statistics; and National Police Agency, Number of suicides)

Moral Hazard and Firefighting

Japan held off surgery till patients' conditions turn critical and operation theaters could be set up. However, there have been cases in abroad where surgery started before operation theaters were set up.

For example, the International Monetary Fund recommended in 1997 that Indonesia wind down 16 distressed banks immediately, even though a proper safety net had not been in place. The implementation of this recommendation resulted in a major bank run and a systemic meltdown in a country that had no major imbalances before the crisis.

The European leaders announced in October 2011 a package that included a Europe-wide stress test on one hand and a government guarantee of bank term funding and reactivation of national capital injection schemes on the other. They must have intended to prepare operation theaters and conduct surgeries simultaneously. However, the sequence was different when implemented: the stress test went out first, the reactivation of capital injection schemes followed in some countries, and the guarantee was substituted later by the European Central Bank's long-term refinancing operation. If proper sequencing had been taken as initially planned, the crisis would not have posed such existential threat to Euro as seen in late 2011 and early 2012.

This contrasts with the US sequence in late 2008 and early 2009. The US authorities guaranteed bank debts in October 2008, installed a capital injection program in February 2009, and then published the results of stress tests in May 2009. However, this perhaps could not have happened without the devastating experience of letting Lehman Brothers go in September 2008. It would have been ideal if the guarantee and capital injection program was installed first, stress testing done next, and then Lehman was resolved in an orderly manner.

Japan's case in the 1990s can be considered as slow actions with proper sequencing. The Indonesian case in 1998 and the European case in 2011 can be characterized as quick actions without proper sequencing. The US case in 2008 and 2009 may be considered as a major improper sequencing (Lehman) followed by quick actions with proper sequencing (stress tests).

These episodes seem to imply the need to combine proper framework for problem recognition and policy responses with effective safety nets. The United States and the European Union, however, significantly cut back their resolution toolkits or put strong constraints on the use of them after they overcame the Global Financial Crisis. They thought if the bailout options stayed on, banks would expect they would be rescued again and would act recklessly.[10]

Following recommendation of the Financial Stability Board, Japan introduced a framework to resolve banks without using public funds, or so-called bail-in approaches, in 2013. Even after that, however, Japan maintained the bailout options introduced in 1998. The International Monetary Fund did not like this and recommended Japan to impose clearer constraints on the use of bailout tools.[11]

Japanese authority rebutted that the newly designed bail-in tools were yet to be tested in real life, and that, though the bail-in approaches may deal with an idiosyncratic failure of a bank, the world had to solve many issues before the approach become capable to address a system-wide distress involving multiple internationally active systemic banks. Japan had to choose between too-little-too-late and a systemic meltdown in the 1990s due to the lack of a robust safety net, and it was premature to discard tested tools acquired at great costs in the 1990s at least while the world is still on the journey to end too-big-to-fail.[12]

Several factors may explain the difference between the choices made by Japan and by Europe and the United States. First, Japan formed a national consensus on the need to use public funds in exceptional cases of systemic distress through the protracted nationwide debate in the 1990s. On the other hand, perhaps the period between the outbreak of the Global Financial Crisis and the bailout of systemic banks in the 2000s was too short to form a national consensus in Europe or in the United States.

Second, Japan addressed the moral hazard issues by arresting 44 former CEOs, 63 non-CEO executives, and 27 staff members of 37 failed financial institutions[13] and by pursuing criminal responsibility of 460 debtors for disturbing the debt collection. It also sued 490 bankers on their civil responsibility.[14] On the other hand, no CEOs of US major banks went to jail after the Global Financial Crisis.

Third, the Japanese bank CEOs' remunerations were much more modest compared to their western counterparts' astronomical bonuses, both before and after the crisis. It was thus easier for the Japanese authority to persuade the nation that the bailout was not to save bankers but to keep banking function for the national economy.

During a systemic crisis, multiple negative feedback loops can be triggered and exceed the capacity for the market to revert to an efficient equilibrium. As the economist Irving Fisher (1933) argued, a ship under ordinary conditions is always near stable equilibrium, but no longer has the ability to return to equilibrium after being tipped beyond a certain angle—instead, it has a tendency to depart further from it.

These negative feedback loops can exist between banks and other banks, between banks and the money and capital markets, between the financial system and the real economy, between the banking system and public finance, and even between the economy and politics. They work through interbank exposures; declines in market liquidity, fire sales, and asset price declines; panic and runs on deposits and other claims; credit crunch, recession, and increased credit costs; and economic performance, confidence in political leadership, and the nation's capability to decide on painful measures in a timely manner.

Overemphasis on these possibilities can work to dissuade painful corrective actions needed to rebuild longer-term resilience of the system. After all, any backstop measures can only buy time and cannot sustain the system forever. The IMF caution on lax use of bailout tools has strong reasons.

At the same time, we should avoid being trapped by politically nice commitments made in peace time and miss opportunities to act promptly with proper sequencing.

In 1999, Tim Geithner and other staff members of the US Treasury compiled "Rubin Doctrine of International Finance," drawing from the Treasury secretary's words and deeds during the Mexican and Asian financial crises.[15] The doctrine maintains that the only certainty in life is that nothing is ever certain. Accordingly, "Optionality is good in itself." It recognizes that "markets are good, but they are not the solution to all problems." Then how can the public sector address problems which markets cannot solve? The doctrine goes, "Money is no substitute for strong policy, but there are times when it is more costly to provide too little money than to provide too much."

An effective crisis management framework should be equipped with a range of options and enough monetary firepower so that it can contain a crisis beyond markets' self-healing capability. It should incorporate a procedure which can provide flexibility and agility, while ensuring proportionate, accountable, and disciplined use of options. The framework should also ensure that the time bought by money will be used to implement strong policy to address root causes of the crisis and restitute function and discipline of good financial markets.

Notes

1. Many of the descriptions of the incidents on November 26, 1997, in this chapter rely on Nishino (2019).
2. Nishino (2019).
3. Nakai, H. (2002).
4. The government first grants government bonds to the Deposit Insurance Corporation and, as the needs to use funds occur, the Corporation will have the bonds repaid by the government.
5. Nakai, S. (2002).
6. The amended Banking Law and the newly enacted Financial Revitalization Law introduced similar but different disclosure obligations in 1998.
7. Gomi (2012).
8. Bank of Japan, Short-term economic survey of enterprises (*Tankan* survey). Responses by companies of all sizes and all industries and on the current condition.
9. Based on search results from the Nikkei Telecon database.
10. For more on this, see G30 Working Group (2018).
11. International Monetary Fund (2017).
12. See, for example, Mori (2017), who was the commissioner of the JFSA at the time of the speech.
13. Some of those who created bad loans and hid losses escaped charges due to statute of limitations and their successors were charged. Some of the arrested were convicted innocent later at the court.
14. Okuyama and Murayama (2019) and Deposit Insurance Corporation of Japan (2007).
15. Rubin and Weisberg (2003).

References

Deposit Insurance Corporation of Japan (Yokin Hoken Kikou). (2007). *Responses to the financial crisis in the Heisei era (Heisei kin'yuu kiki eno taiou)*. Kin'yuu Zaisei Jijou Kenkyuukai.

Economic Planning Agency. (1999). *Annual report on the Japanese Economy for 1999 (Heisei 11 nendo ban keizai hakusho)*.

Fisher, I. (1933). The debt-deflation theory of great depressions. *Econometrica: Journal of the Econometric Society, 1*(4), 337–357.

Gomi, H. (2012). *Financial system turbulence: A monologue by a JFSA commissioner (Kin'yuu douran: Kin'yuuchou choukan no dokuhaku)*. Nihon Keizai Shinbun Shuppansha.

G30 Working Group. (2018). *Managing the next financial crisis: An assessment of emergency arrangements in the major economies*. Group of Thirty.

International Monetary Fund. (2017). *Japan financial system stability assessment* (IMF Country Report No. 17/244).
Mori, N. (2017). A brake pedal alone cannot guarantee safety. In Financial Services Agency. (2018). *From static regulation to dynamic supervision: Speeches by Commissioner Nobuchika Mori*.
Motonishi, T., & Yoshikawa, H. (1999). Causes of the Long Stagnation of Japan during the 1990s: Financial or real? *Journal of the Japanese and International Economies, 13*(3), 181–200.
Nakai, H. (2002). *Clear, cloudy, starry, and rainy (Sei yin sei u)*. Misuzu-shobo.
Nakai, S. (2002). *Squint eyed views on the financial sector policy (Yabunirami kin'yuu gyosei)*. Zaikei-shoho.
Nakaso, H. (2001). *The financial crisis in Japan during the 1990s: How the Bank of Japan responded and the lessons learnt* (BIS Papers No. 6).
Nishino T. (2019). *Financial history of the Heisei era (Heisei kin'yuu shi)*. Chukoshinsho.
Okuyama, T., & Murayama, O. (2019). *Deep inside the incidents of the bubble economy (Baburu keizai jiken no shinso)*. Iwanami-shinsho.
Rubin, R., & Weisberg, J. (2003). *In an uncertain world*. New York: Random House.
Suzuki, T. (2009). *The extinction of a mammoth bank: Testimony of the last CEO of the LTCB 10 years after (Kyodai Ginko no Shometsu: Chogin Saigo no Todori 10 nenme no Shogen)*. Toyo-keizai.

Open Access This chapter is licensed under the terms of the Creative Commons Attribution-NonCommercial-NoDerivatives 4.0 International License (http://creativecommons.org/licenses/by-nc-nd/4.0/), which permits any noncommercial use, sharing, distribution and reproduction in any medium or format, as long as you give appropriate credit to the original author(s) and the source, provide a link to the Creative Commons license and indicate if you modified the licensed material. You do not have permission under this license to share adapted material derived from this chapter or parts of it.

The images or other third party material in this chapter are included in the chapter's Creative Commons license, unless indicated otherwise in a credit line to the material. If material is not included in the chapter's Creative Commons license and your intended use is not permitted by statutory regulation or exceeds the permitted use, you will need to obtain permission directly from the copyright holder.

CHAPTER 6

Restructuring Banks and Borrowers

Abstract The systemic banking crisis subsided by March 1999, but it took five more painful years before the Japanese banking system recovered full health. This chapter reviews the process to restructure banks and borrowers and the impacts the process had on the labor force. It then tries to estimate the costs borne by corporates, banks, and taxpayers and explore what would have been the consequence if the immediate clean-up option had been chosen in 1992.

Keywords Bad loans · Bank resolution · Corporate restructuring · Debt overhang · Unviable firms · Japanese employment · Resolution costs

By the end of March 1999, major banks had been recapitalized, and the safety net had been much strengthened. Bad loans were better provisioned against, and the regulator was revamped. With these, the systemic meltdown was averted, but the Japanese banking system had a long way to go before recovering its full health.

Figure 6.1 describes the key elements of the complications which were at work. Even after their decade-long decline, the asset prices did not stabilize and continued to impair the balance sheets of real estate developers and construction firms. In addition, the recession in the late 1990s made manufacturers and retailers run losses. By the turn of the

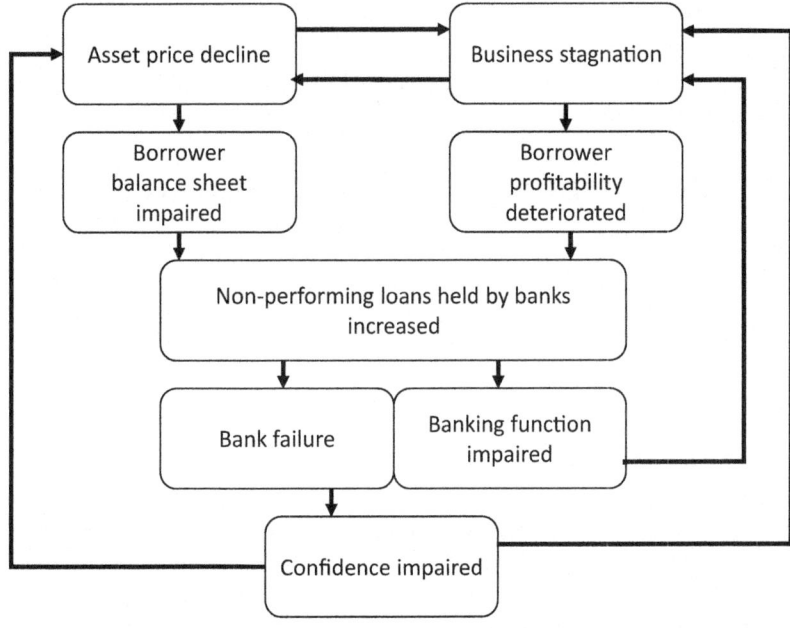

Fig. 6.1 Persistent vicious cycle (*Source* Author's illustration)

millennium, bad loans were mushrooming through both i) the traditional channel of borrower balance sheet impairment due to asset price falls and ii) the new channel of borrower profitability deterioration due to economic stagnation.

Every year, banks declared that they thoroughly looked at bad loans and disclosed them all, but they had to report much more in the following year. Market participants naturally suspected that regulators and bankers were hiding more problems.

Banks loaded with bad loans did not have much capacity to take additional risks. Bankers were busy dealing with existing borrowers with difficulties. Lending to new promising borrowers was clogged, prolonging stagnation. Borrowers were scared by the credit crunch in 1998 and had become cautious in making new investments.

Increased credit costs made banks fail, and big black headlines reporting new bank failures impaired public confidence in bankers and regulators, even though depositors were fully protected by the new safety nets. These developments in turn further pushed down asset prices and business activities.

Initially, many hoped that, if the asset prices stop declining and economic activities pick up, the vicious cycle would be reversed. Despite the enormous fiscal and monetary stimulus, however, the reversal had not happened even after a decade.

By summer 1998, it was widely recognized that cleaning up of bank and borrower balance sheets were needed to sever the vicious cycle and reactivate the economy. The cleaning up, however, was never easy. The JFSA tightened the standards, set new targets, repeated intensive on-site inspections, improved the mechanisms for borrower restructuring, and resolved numerous banks. But it took five more painful years to finally clean up the problem.

Resolving Bad Loans

From 1998 to 2003, the JFSA[1] conducted three waves of on-site inspections to expose bad loans held by banks and to urge their early resolution.

The first wave of inspections was carried out from July 1998 to May 1999. The JFSA, in cooperation with regional finance bureaus of the Ministry of Finance and the Bank of Japan, conducted a Focused Inspection of loan books of all the 143 banks. Inspectors identified more bad loans than bankers did, and banks recognized a record credit loss for the fiscal year 1998. In the second quarter of 1999, 31 banks, *shinkin* banks, and credit cooperatives were resolved.

After the Focused Inspection, the scope of the review was expanded from asset quality to banks' internal processes including governance, compliance, and risk management. The Inspection Manual published in July 1999 incorporated a comprehensive checklist covering all such areas and guided the review. The number of the inspectors at the JFSA headquarters grew from 164 in March 1999 to 319 in March 2001 and those at the local offices grew from 456 to 567 during the same period.

The amount of bad loans, however, continued to increase even after the Focused Inspection. To put an end to the problem, the economic policy package published by the government in April 2001 requested banks to remove existing bad loans from their balance sheets within two years and new bad loans within three years ("2-year and 3-year rule"). Major banks were requested to disclose the progress and the JFSA was to monitor it.

On the other hand, the short economic remission came to an end by September 2001. The GDP growth rate of the second quarter of 2001, published in September, turned negative. Nikkei Stock Price Index, which had been above 20,000 yen in March 2000, fell below 10,000 yen.

Confidence in the banking system was particularly impaired when a large supermarket group failed in September 2001. Bonds issued by the group had traded much below par, but banks had not classified loans to the group as doubtful. This incident strengthened market participants' suspicion that banks hided large amount of doubtful loans.

Responding to this, in the economic policy package in October 2001, the government declared that the bad loan problem shall be rectified within three years and announced that the JFSA would conduct a Special Inspection that focused on loans to large borrowers on which the capital market was signaling doubts.

This second wave of asset quality review was conducted between October 2001 and April 2002. In ordinary inspections, inspectors review bankers' assessments of the loan book after the annual financial statements are published. In this case, inspectors discussed with major banks how their large borrowers should be classified and provisioned concurrently with the process to produce the financial statements for the fiscal year 2001, which ended in March 2002. While the Special Inspection went on, 45 banks, *shinkin* banks, and credit cooperatives were resolved.

Gomi (2012), who was the director general of the JFSA's Inspection Bureau, recounts that he felt clear changes in bankers' mindsets by the end of 2001. One former inspector recalls that, when he did the Focused Inspection in 1998, major banks did not allocate quality human resource to the task of bad loan resolution, but that they started to treat the task as top priority around the time of the 2001 Special Inspection.

As shown in Fig. 6.2, both the disclosed amount of bad loans and the credit losses recognized by banks jumped up in March 2002. Further, the JFSA in April 2002 requested major banks to eliminate 50% of doubtful loans from their balance sheet within a year from the time classified as doubtful and 80% within two years ("50% and 80% rule"). Combined with the "2-year and 3-year rule," the outstanding amount of bad loans should start to decline.

But the prime minister could not wait to see if these policies would work as envisaged. He replaced the minister for financial services in September 2002. The new minister, Takenaka Heizo, openly denied the approach adopted by his predecessor, Yanagisawa Hakuo, who directed

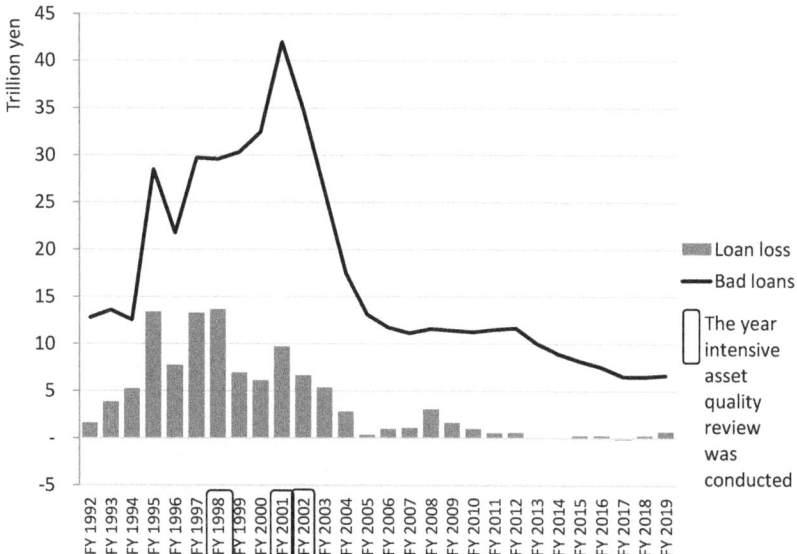

Fig. 6.2 Bad loans held by banks and loan losses incurred (*Source* Financial Services Agency, Disclosures according to the Financial Revitalization Act made for the accounting year ending in March 2020 (Reiwa 2 nen 3 gatsu ki ni okeru Kinyuu Saisei Hou kaiji saiken no joukyou tou), August 2020)

the Focused Inspection in 1998 and the Special Inspection in 2001. Responding to the criticism that his policy would lead to a hard-landing rather than a soft-landing, Takenaka (2008) argued "the policies taken so far have been 'never-landing' (i.e. never arriving at a solution), and those would lead in the long run to a 'crush landing' for the economy." In his view, the JFSA "was paralyzed by a sort of functional failure" and the JFSA bureaucrats "were prisoners of the idea of bureaucratic infallibility (the public demonstration of an attitude implying that all the policies adopted so far have been impeccable)."

His confrontation with big banks was highly publicized. Takenaka (2008) recounts about the press conference the CEOs of big banks jointly held in October: "When my staff members and I watched the proceedings of the press conference, we were struck with the clear realization that we could 'win' this. The players who had created the non-performing loans in the first place, and who were now causing so much trouble for the Japanese people, were now seen in a position opposing the reforms. Moreover, the sight of the bank presidents grouped together at the press conference like a bunch of incompetents, fully exposing buddy-buddy group consciousness left over from the days of the old convoy system, was a graphic indication of the lack of governance at the current banks, as well as their lack of strategy. The public would never support such banks – I was convinced of that."

One month after taking office, Minister Takenaka and his team published a new policy package. The package set the goal of cutting major banks' bad loan ratio by half by March 2005. To attain the goal, the package announced that (i) the discount cash flow approach shall be used in provisioning against doubtful loans, (ii) inspectors shall require major banks to adopt consistent classifications of large problem borrowers, and (iii) the JFSA shall disclose the aggregate amount of gaps between bankers' own assessment and inspectors' review and issue administrative sanctions on banks if the gap persists unreasonably. With these sticks in hands, the JFSA inspectors conducted another round of Special Inspection from January to April 2003.

While waiting for the outcome of the Special Inspection, the whole Japanese economy was in suspense. As the 50–80% rule introduced by the former minister Yanagisawa was still alive, majority of the borrowers newly classified as doubtful had to be restructured or resolved within a year or two. Speculations on imminent bankruptcies of large zombie firms were hazarded, and, on April 28, 2003, the Nikkei Stock Price Index hit the record low of 7604 yen, the level almost half of the bottom seen during the 1998 crisis. Some also speculated that some of the major banks may turn insolvent. The fear of another systemic crisis prevailed.

However, banks' annual reports published by the end of May 2003 showed that, despite the enhanced scrutiny, the amount of bad loans declined. The amount of credit losses, measured using the discount cash flow approach, was also lower. In other words, this round of Special Inspection underscored that the preceding round had already properly identified bad loans and loan losses. At the same time, the new minister's highly confrontational discourse worked to convince the market that no forbearance was exercised and gave strong credibility to this outcome. The capital adequacy of one major bank, Resona Bank, dipped below the regulatory minimum, but, as described below, the government gave a precautionary capital injection, avoiding wipe-off of the shareholders' rights and dissipating the fear of another systemic crisis.

Stock prices were reversed. An economic boom started in the United States gave the Japanese economy a long-awaited stimulus. The real GDP, which was almost flat in 2001 and 2002, resumed growth at an annual rate of around 2%. The bad loan ratio of major banks continued to decline from 8.4% in March 2002 and reached 2.9% in March 2005, overachieving the goal of halving, and stayed at the low level since then. In FY 2005, the Japanese banks incurred almost no credit losses in aggregate. The six large city commercial land price index, which had continued to decline for 15 years, started to pick up in March 2005. The vicious cycle described in Fig. 6.1 was reversed, and finally came the long-awaited reverse Minsky moment.

The initiative taken by Minister Takenaka has been among the most controversial of the financial sector policies adopted in Japan. In the view of Gomi (2012), who served both Yanagisawa and Takenaka at the JFSA, "The directions pursued by the two ministers were by no means contradictory. The approach adopted by Minister Yanagisawa in fact did not allow banks to take time or to proceed on their own speed." On the other hand, Takemori (2009) argues, "It was, after all, the matter of confidence. . . . It was absolutely necessary for someone to demonstrate that the problem was finally and irrevocably resolved, using means everyone could clearly understand." When the US authorities conducted stress tests in early 2009 and put an end to the crisis of confidence, some commentators in Japan compared this with the shock treatment administered in Japan six years before.

Resolving Banks

During this financial cycle, 181 banks, *shinkin* banks, and credit cooperatives were resolved. Of which, 63 were resolved before the full sets of resolution tools were installed in October 1998. The authority had to painstakingly craft and tailor ways to protect depositors for each individual case.

At the time of the introduction of the full safety net, the plan was to clean up non-viable banks by March 2001 and to reinstall a ceiling on deposit protection in April. The ruling parties considered the reinstallment premature and postponed it by one year, and the JFSA largely completed the clean-up job by the new deadline of March 2002, resolving 117 institutions.

Minister Yanagisawa directed the resolution of 99 institutions. During the last quarter of 2001, the frequency of failures reached three in one week. Each and every resolution was accompanied by strong political and social repercussions and technical and operational challenges, but no systemic disruptions or runs occurred.

His successor, Minister Takenaka, had to handle two high profile cases, one of a major nationwide bank and the other of a key regional bank. The capital adequacy of the former, Resona Bank, dipped below the regulatory minimum, and the government injected 2 trillion yen of capital and replaced the management in May 2003. The latter, Ashikaga Bank, was found to be of negative net worth. The government nationalized it in November 2003 and nominated a new CEO. The systemic risk clauses of the Deposit Insurance Law (the last two columns of Table 5.1) were applied to these cases, as Resona was judged systemic to the national economy, and Ashikaga, to the regional economy. There has been no bank failure since then, except for one idiosyncratic case.

Restructuring Borrowers

Bad loans for banks are excess debts for distressed borrowers. Banks have four options: (i) to continue to lend and provision against the loans, (ii) to work with the borrowers and help them resurrect by restructuring their business models and balance sheets, (iii) to trigger liquidation procedures and receive proceeds, or (iv) to sell loans to new investors. The way banks resolve bad loans determine the fates of the distressed borrowers, their employees, suppliers, customers, and the national and regional economy.

During the in-between years, the Japanese banks largely chose the first option to provision against potential losses without addressing borrowers and wait till the borrowers fail or recover. The drawback of this approach had long been known: It can harm banks as banks tend to incur further losses year after year if the asset prices continue to decline or the borrowers continue to run losses. Bankers will be occupied with monitoring distressed borrowers and may not be able to focus on more promising borrowers.

In addition, perhaps more importantly, such an approach can also damage borrowers and the economy through two channels: debt overhang and delayed exit of unviable firms.

First, debt overhang. According to Myers (1977), the book value of a company refers to assets already in place, whereas a significant part of firms' market values comes from the present value of future growth opportunities, which can be realized only if the company makes further discretionary investments. He showed that the existence of corporate debt can reduce the latter by weakening the corporation's incentive to undertake good future investments.

Suppose Company A had a factory and engineers which can adapt to future changes in technology and demands, and a major part of the company's value consisted of the growth opportunity, not of assets in place. Also suppose that, in the late 1980s, the company invested in a commercial real estate using money borrowed from banks, and by mid-1990s, the company was with much bigger debts than the value of its assets in place. Banks hesitated to lend more to finance new investments, frustrating the growth opportunity and impairing the core of the corporate value. In the early 2000s, the main bank kept large bad loans to the company, and the company had the factory, which was already obsolete, and the commercial real estate, whose market value was one tenth of the acquisition price, on the asset side of its balance sheet.

But what if the banks and the company could work together to eliminate this debt overhang by dividing the company into two, one taking over engineers with the factory on the asset side and some debts and some equity converted from debts on the liability side, and the other with the commercial real estate on the asset side and the large debts on the liability side? The latter has to be liquidated and the bank will surely incur losses, but both the company and the bank can avoid losing the value of the growth opportunity.

Second, delayed exit of unviable firms. Even if a company is currently with negative net worth or the current cashflow is insufficient to cover market rate interest payments, it still may be viable if it has a sound business model. By surviving a temporary adverse economic condition, by restructuring debts, or by shifting its business lines, it could be turned around. But firms are unviable if they lack sustainable business plans.[2]

Suppose Company B, which dominated the global market, invested in a big factory in the late 1980s, financing it by loans extended by banks. Competition with manufacturers based in other Asian economies intensified in the 1990s, and the company sold the products at prices which barely covered the variable costs but were totally inadequate to cover the fixed costs. It ran losses every year and could not embark on efforts to rebuild its competitiveness, but the bank, rather than to recognize a big loss writing off the whole loan, continued to lend and kept this unviable firm alive.

If the banks and the company could work together to wind down the company in an orderly manner, perhaps the banks could limit the ultimate size of the loan losses. Precious engineers, skilled workers, and any competent managers could be freed up from inefficient use and mobilized to build a new business model. New entrants may bring in animal spirits and new ideas and technology. The productivity of the Japanese economy could be enhanced.

In both cases, the second scenario looks better, but to make right choices, one needs to distinguish promising losers from unviable firms. Misdiagnosis could turn worse than wait and see approach: If we wind down the former, the valuable seeds of growth are prematurely killed. If we restructure the debts of the latter, we will be proactively delaying the exit of unviable firms.

During the golden age of what Aoki and Patrick (1995) called the Japanese main bank system, it was one of the key function of the main bank to make such judgments and administer restructuring or orderly winding down. There were many legendary cases in the Japanese economic history: Teikoku Bank saved Toyota in 1949, the Industrial Bank of Japan reconstructed Nissan Motor Co. and Nissan Chemicals in the 1950s and 60s, and Sumitomo Bank restructured Mazda in the 1970s and resurrected Asahi Beer in the 1980s. Without main banks, we would not see Lexus or Super Dry, much-loved national beer, today.

The task performed by main banks during the period of rapid economic growth, however, was much easier than the task to be performed in the post-bubble era. Previously most major companies had big growth opportunities, but, after the collapse of the bubbles, economy stagnated, and many borrowers' growth opportunities turned questionable. Before the financial deregulations in the 1980s, a main bank had close ties with borrowers, which helped monitoring them, but the relationship had been much weakened since then. Banks' high profitability and accumulated latent gains in the equity portfolio helped them withstand temporary costs to be incurred in restructuring borrowers, but such financial clout was almost depleted during the 1990s. Although main banks continued to perform central roles in addressing many of the distressed borrowers, a mechanism which can complement main banks' role had to be created to implement effective corporate resolution and restructuring.

Indeed, such need had long been recognized. Chicken and egg problems, however, persisted: Banks did not sell bad loans as there were no secondary market, and the market did not develop as banks did not sell. Corporate restructuring professionals could not accumulate experience as there were only limited cases, and corporate restructuring did not proceed as there were few experienced experts. There also was a first mover problem: When multiple banks lend to a borrower, the bank which initiated restructuring tended to bear bigger burden. Moreover, the existing corporate resolution processes focused on liquidation, were rigid, and took many years to complete.

Enormous efforts had been taken to create private and public agents who can administer restructuring. New agents born during the post-crisis phase include the following:

- Loan servicers: Amid the crisis in 1998, interested congressmen submitted a bill to make it possible to establish companies specialized in the business to collect loans for financial institutions or to purchase loans from them, the business which had been allowed only for lawyers. The Law on Loan Servicers was enacted in the year. The amount of loans serviced by loan servicers stayed at around 10 trillion yen in 1999 and 2000 but, as a result of the regulator's push to eliminate bad loans from bank balance sheets, jumped to 30 trillion yen in 2001 and stayed at the level till 2010.
- The Resolution and Collection Corporation (RCC): The RCC had purchased bad loans from failed *Jusen* and banks, but its role was expanded in 2001 so that it can purchase from sound banks as well. The government instructed the RCC to judge if a borrower had a potential for recovery or not, and restructure and revitalize those with potential and rigorously collect from those without. The RCC purchased 3 trillion yen of bad loans from sound banks at the price of 0.3 trillion yen and revitalized around 700 borrowers.
- The Industrial Revitalization Corporation of Japan (IRCJ): A special law to establish the IRCJ was enacted in April 2003 and the Corporation started its business in May, with two years to decide which companies to revitalize and up to five years before exit. The IRCJ resurrected 41 borrowers, whose initial liabilities amounted to 4 trillion yen, or around one quarter of the substandard loans held by

banks at the time of the IRCJ's start. It made profit amounting to 125 billion yen and, more importantly, released corps of experienced corporate turnaround professionals to the private sector by the time it was disbanded in 2007.
- SME Business Rehabilitation Support Co-operatives: In 2003, based on the revised Law on Special Measures for Industrial Revitalization, SME Business Rehabilitation Support Co-operatives were established in all prefectures. The co-operatives provide advice to small and medium size enterprises (SMEs) and conduct initial discussion with lenders without charging the SMEs. If the SMEs so wish, the co-operatives prepare restructuring plans, coordinate with lenders, and support implementation of the plans. Each year during its early periods, the Co-operatives provided advice to around 3000 SMEs and produced more than 400 restructuring plans.

Procedural improvements were also made.

- In 2000, the Civil Rehabilitation Law was enacted, and an in-court process simpler and more flexible than the process under the Composition Law, which the new law replaced, was introduced. The number of cases of restructuring-oriented court process jumped from 225 in FY 1999 to 769 in FY 2000.
- In 2002, the Corporate Reorganization Act was wholly revamped to make restructuring process for large corporate more efficient, prompt, and effective.
- In addition, the Guidelines for Multi-Creditor Out-of-Court Workout was produced by a group of interested lawyers and representatives of bankers' associations and business associations in 2001. The guidelines standardized workout steps for troubled companies to be taken in out-of-court processes led by main banks.

The supervisory pressures to make banks remove bad loans from their balance sheet, new players such as loan servicers, the RCC, the IRCJ, and the SME Business Rehabilitation Support Co-operatives, together with the new processes like the Civil Rehabilitation and the Multi-Creditor Out-of-Court Workout, all emerged around the turn of the millennium, worked together to attain simultaneous resolution of bad loan problems and excess debt problems.

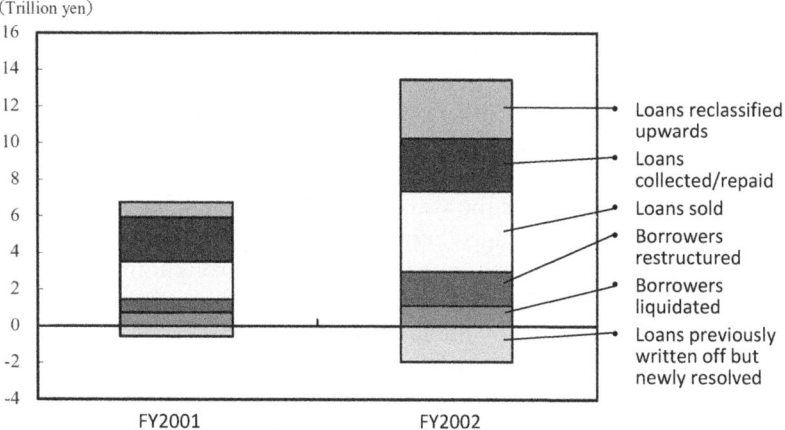

Fig. 6.3 Composition of the loans categorized doubtful or worse and removed from the balance sheets of major banks (*Source* Cabinet Office [2003], with legend translated by the author)

According to Cabinet Office (2003), the amount of doubtful or worse loans removed from the balance sheets of major banks jumped from 6 trillion yen in FY 2001 to 12 trillion yen in FY 2002 (Fig. 6.3). Of the 12 trillion yen, around 2 trillion yen was the result of the restructuring of the borrowers administered in court. Around 3 trillion yen was resulted from the loans being reclassified upwards, of which 43% was the outcome of out-of-court restructuring processes. But for the enhancements in actors and processes, many more borrowers might have been simply liquidated.

Labor Market Adjustments

The Corporate Japan did not resort to massive layoffs during the recessions, and the Japanese labor market never saw such high unemployment rates Europe and the United States saw after the Global Financial Crisis. The Japanese employment system, with some modifications, survived throughout the financial cycle. But the youth and women bore larger share of the adjustment burden than the traditional incumbents of the Japanese lifetime employment system, and the effects persisted even after the recovery of the economy.

During the in-between years, the unemployment rate steadily rose from around 2% to around 3.5%. The 1998 crisis pushed it up by one percentage point to around 4.5%, and the wave of corporate liquidation and restructuring in 2001–2002 raised it by another one percentage point to around 5.5%. The unemployment rate then gradually declined to the pre-crisis level of around 3.5% by mid-2007.

Pain was more acute for the younger generation. The unemployment rate among the population aged between 15 and 24, which was at around 4.5% in the early 1990s, continued to climb up throughout the 1990s and came close to 11% in the first half of 2002. The ratio then gradually declined to around 7% by the first half of 2008. So-called "job-search ice age," during which new graduates had particular difficulty in finding jobs as lifetime employees, is said to have started in the mid-1990s and have come to an end in the mid-2000s. The cohort which entered the job market during the period, or the "ice-age generation," continued to be disadvantaged. Genda, Kondo, and Ohta (2010) found the negative effects of the unemployment rate at graduation on subsequent employment and earnings are much more persistent in Japan than in the United States.

The core incumbents of the Japanese employment system had their lifetime employment protected, while other groups of employees saw significant deterioration in their job security. Kambayashi and Kato (2017) show that the ten-year job retention rate did not change much for the traditionally priviliged core group of employees, or male regular employees with college degree and at least five-year employment history at the same employer, in spite of the banking crisis and the ensuing corporate restructuring. But the job retention rate for those outside the group significantly declined after 1998.

The seniority-based wage system, where the wage level is a function of the number of years worked at the company, stayed, but the wage for employees in their fifties, a symbol of employers' appreciation of employees' loyalty, was significantly reduced.

Between 1997 and 2002, the ratio of "regular employees" (those who are expected to have lifetime employment, on-the-job training, and seniority-based wage) in the population changed little for men aged 18–70 from 60 to 59%, but for women and the youth (age 22–30), the decline was significant, from 26 to 22% for women and 61 to 54% for the youth (Kambayashi and Kato 2016).

The Cabinet Office (2009) found that the growth in the ratio of non-regular employees and the increase in income inequality were particularly pronounced between 1997 and 2002, and that the recovery of income of the lower-income group was much slower than that of the mid- or high-income groups during the economic recovery between 2002 and 2008.

The corporate Japan hired more women, youth, and elderly as non-regular employees with lower costs, and continuously reduced the wage share. This helped the corporate sector accumulate financial surplus at a level equivalent to around 4% of the GDP almost every year since 1999, as we will see in the next chapter (Fig. 7.1).

How Much Did It Cost?

The first line of defense against the shocks arising from the asset price collapse is corporate sector's profits and capital. Between FY 1992 and 2004, the non-financial corporate sector recognized 284 trillion yen of non-recurring losses. Corporations incur non-recurring losses even without bubbles, but its sharp rise in the latter half of the 1990s (Fig. 6.4, broken line) suggests that significant part of them should have come from impairments in the values of assets held.

Part of the losses was covered by non-recurring profits (dotted line), including those realized by selling assets with latent gains. The gap between the non-recurring losses and profits, shown by the double line, amounted to 112 trillion yen in total. As non-recurring losses and non-recurring profits may stay with different companies, however, not all of the latter are available to cover the former. Uncovered non-recurring losses still may be covered by annual ordinary profits and corporations' own capital, but to the extent it could not be covered, banks' claim to the corporations would be impaired, except for the portion compensated by public loan guarantee schemes.

The single line in Fig. 6.4 shows the amount of credit loss recognized by banks. The line, which moved a few years earlier than the double line,

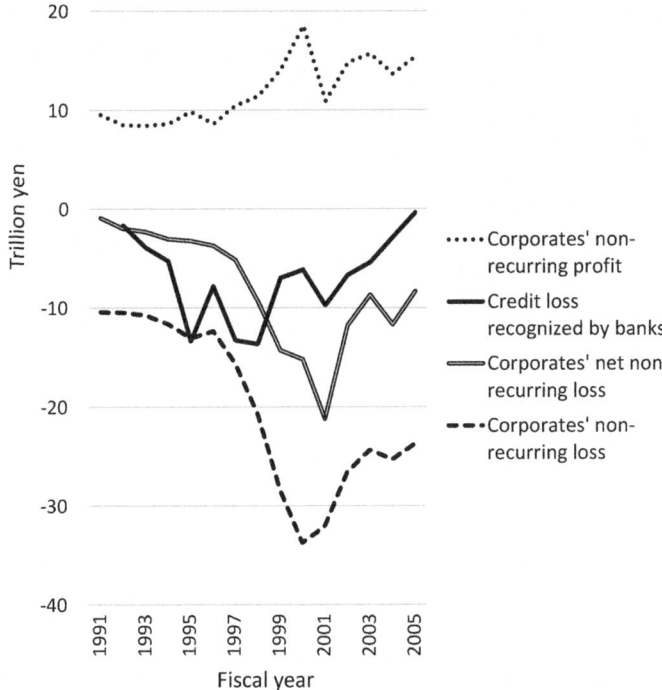

Fig. 6.4 Corporate non-recurring profit/loss and credit cost to banks (*Source* Ministry of Finance, Financial Statements Statistics of Corporations by Industry; Financial Services Agency, Disclosures according to the Financial Revitalization Act made for the accounting year ending in March 2020 (Reiwa 2 nen 3 gatsu ki ni okeru Kin'yuu Saisei Hou kaiji saiken no joukyou tou), August 2020)

seems to imply that banks provisioned against anticipated losses. Aggregate amount of credit losses reached 96 trillion yen. Banks incur credit losses even during their ordinary course of business, but majority of this extraordinary level of losses may be attributed to the bubbles and their busts. Banks partly covered them by realizing the latent gain in banks' equity portfolio and by annual ordinary profits. To the extent the credit losses could not be covered, banks' own capital was depleted.

The Deposit Insurance Corporation injected 12 trillion yen of capital to undercapitalized banks, which was, in aggregate, recovered with profits. However, it had to pay additional 19 trillion yen to resolve failed banks. Part of the resolution cost was recovered by deposit insurance premium, but the residual 10 trillion yen was borne by taxpayers.

Running the risk of oversimplification, it may be said that the collapse of the bubble resulted in capital loss to the corporate sector amounting to 60% of the annual GDP (284 trillion yen), credit cost to banks amounting to 20% (96 trillion yen), bank resolution cost to the deposit insurance amounting to 4% (19 trillion yen), and direct cost to taxpayers amounting to 2% (10 trillion yen). These are the direct financial costs only. Bigger costs accrued to all members of the society in the form of lost revenues due to economic stagnation.

What if the Immediate Clean-Up Option Had Been Chosen in 1992?

As seen in Chapter 4, the Bank of Japan and Prime Minister Miyazawa in 1992 tried to enhance the public backstop and quickly clean up the problems in the banking system. In the real world, their view did not prevail, but what if the immediate clean-up option had been chosen in 1992?

Given the complexity of the matter, no counterfactual can be reliable even minimally, but it might still be of some interest to try a wild speculation. If we are to assume the consequence of the immediate clean-up could be like a fast-forwarded version of the real history, a counterfactual may look as follows:

> Banks continued to deny the problem, and the proposal to introduce a strong public backstop was rejected by the public and the Diet. To demonstrate the need for a backstop, the Ministry of Finance and the Bank of Japan ran special inspections and then disclosed the true magnitude of the problem.
>
> The stock price collapsed as was the case in April 2003. Latent gains on banks' equity portfolios turned to latent losses, and large part of the Japanese banking system was found undercapitalized or insolvent.
>
> Rating agencies downgraded Japanese banks, funding in overseas markets became unavailable, and the Japanese banks, still among the largest in the world, started fire sales of their dollar-denominated assets abroad, turning the global financial markets into turmoil. The US authorities provided a

friendly advice to their Japanese counterparts that a strong public backstop had to be immediately introduced.

At the same time, as we saw in November 1997, queues were formed in front of bank branches across the country. Blanket deposit protection was declared, and the ruling party decided to introduce public capital injection scheme, as was the case in December 1997. Waves of capital injections, bank resolutions, and the restructuring of borrowers ensued, and bankruptcies, unemployment, and suicide surged as we saw in the wake of the 1998 crisis. Massive public spending was implemented to boost the economy. Responsibilities of relevant bankers and regulators were rigorously pursued.

Would the total costs incurred to non-financial corporations and to banks have been smaller under this scenario? Assuming that the scenario had not resulted in a systemic meltdown with uncontrollable downward spirals, the total cost must have been smaller, as many problems would have been addressed before they exacerbated. Given the size of the problem accumulated over the bubble years, however, the savings might not have been dramatic.

The cost incurred to the non-financial corporate sector was broadly in line with what the sector did during the bubble years. The assets held by the sector grew by 503 trillion yen during the six years between March 1986 and March 1992. The sector bought 123 trillion yen of lands and increased the amount of equities, plant, and equipment on the balance sheets by 141 trillion yen. Compare the sum of the two, 264 trillion yen, with the gross non-recurring losses recognized by the non-financial corporate sector, 284 trillion yen.

Also, the credit cost recognized by banks, 96 trillion yen, may broadly correspond to the size of the problems at the industries which produced bad loans. The real estate industry alone acquired 56 trillion yen of real estate and increased debts to banks by 64 trillion yen during the six years between March 1986 and March 1992 (Fig. 2.3). The construction industry acquired 28 trillion yen of real estates and increased debts to banks by 16 trillion yen. The wholesale and retail distribution industry acquired 57 trillion yen of real estates and increased debts to banks by 32 trillion yen. The three industries alone added to their balance sheets 100 trillion yen of real estates and 112 trillion yen of debts to banks.

On the other hand, the cost would have been much larger should this scenario have resulted in a systemic meltdown, i.e., if the public confidence in the banking system could not be restituted, bank runs continued, and a downward spiral between the banking sector and the real economy was not halted.

Would the risk of a systemic meltdown have been greater under the counterfactual scenario?

As Fig. 6.4 shows, the non-financial corporate sector recognized the problem largely after the 1998 crisis, and thus an early clean up would have meant doing the same just earlier. On the other hand, in the real life, banks already recognized half of the total credit costs during the in-between years and had to address only the remaining half after the crisis. If the crisis should be brought forward to 1992, then the banking system would have been required to address much bigger problem at once than was the case in the real life after 1998.

Perhaps more banks would have been resolved in a shorter period, and that might have increased the risk of operational failure in resolution, resulting in a greater risk of a systemic meltdown. Also, only deposit insurance premiums for fewer years could have been counted on. Taxpayers might have had to cover a larger share of the cost. If a national consensus to spend tens of trillions of yen could not have been formed quickly, then the process would have been more prone to a systemic meltdown.

Would the competitiveness of the Japanese industry have been revived more effectively under this alternative scenario?

Most likely so, so far as we assume no systemic meltdown. The problems arising from debt overhang and delayed exit of unviable firms would have been much smaller. The shock could have been deeper and scarier, and the Corporate Japan could have become more risk-averse right after the shock, but a temporary shock would have imposed less damage on entrepreneurship than pains persisting over a decade. The "job-search ice age" generation, who lost the opportunities to benefit from on-the-job training, would have been produced only for much shorter period.

In short, the quick cleaning-up scenario would have had a good upside potential. It may have resulted in smaller (though still large) financial costs for the non-financial corporate sector and for banks, a sharper but shorter bout in unemployment, and better preservation of entrepreneurship in Japan. But it may have resulted in larger costs for taxpayers, and most importantly, could have triggered a systemic meltdown, with possible spillovers to the global financial system.

Policymakers cannot choose an option on their own unless the risk of triggering an irrecoverable catastrophe is reasonably mitigated. Although a bureaucracy tends to overemphasize the risk, in hindsight there indeed was the risk to see the sum of the two darkest days, November 26, 1997, when depositors' queues were formed across the country, and April 28, 2003, the day the stock prices hit the lowest point, at once. On the other hand, if there had been a strong public backstop already at the time, the quick cleaning-up option could have reduced the overall social costs while limiting the risk of a systemic meltdown, and the benefit may have outweighed the cost of moral hazard possibly produced by the backstop.

Notes

1. In July 2000, the Financial System Planning Bureau of the Ministry of Finance and the Financial Supervisory Agency was merged to form the Financial Services Agency. In January 2001, the Financial Reconstruction Commission was merged into the Financial Services Agency.
2. Here, "unviable firms" are defined by unviability of their business models, not by their current financial conditions. The concept is thus unrelated to what Caballero et al. (2008) call "zombie firms." They call a firm zombie if banks' lending terms to it is more favorable than the prevailing market terms, regardless of the viability of its business model. Nakamura and Fukuda (2013) find that a majority of the zombie firms eventually resuscitated during the first half of the 2000s.

References

Aoki, M., & Patrick, H. (1995). *The Japanese main bank system: Its relevance for developing and transforming economies*. Oxford: Oxford University Press.

Caballero, R. J., Hoshi, T., & Kashyap, A. K. (2008). Zombie lending and depressed restructuring in Japan. *American Economic Review, 98*(5), 1943–1977.

Cabinet Office. (2003). *Annual report on the Japanese economy and public Finance 2003—No gains without reforms II*.

Cabinet Office. (2009). *Annual report on the Japanese economy and public finance 2009—Overcoming financial crisis and vision for sustained recovery*.

Genda, Y., Kondo, A., & Ohta, S. (2010). Long-term effects of a recession at labor market entry in Japan and the United States. *Journal of Human Resources, 45*(1), 157–196.

Gomi, H. (2012). *Financial turmoil, a monologue of an JFSA commissioner (Kin'yuu douran, Kin'yuuchou choukan no dokuhaku)*. Nikkei.

Kambayashi, R., & Kato, T. (2016). *Good jobs and bad jobs in Japan: 1982–2007* (Working Paper Series No. 348). Center on Japanese Economy and Business. Columbia Business School.

Kambayashi, R., & Kato, T. (2017). Long-term employment and job security over the past 25 years: A comparative study of Japan and the United States. *ILR Review, 70*(2), 359–394.

Myers, S. C. (1977). Determinants of corporate borrowing. *Journal of Financial Economics, 5*(2), 147–175.

Nakamura, J., & Fukuda, S. (2013). What happened to "zombie" firms in Japan?: Reexamination for the lost two decades. *Global Journal of Economics, 2*(02), 1350007.

Takenaka, H. (2008). *The structural reforms of the Koizumi Cabinet: An insider's account of the economic revival of Japan.* Tokyo: Nikkei Publishing.

Takemori, S. (2009). *Nine faces of economic crises (Keizai kiki ha kokonotsu no kao wo motsu).* Nikkei BP.

Open Access This chapter is licensed under the terms of the Creative Commons Attribution-NonCommercial-NoDerivatives 4.0 International License (http://creativecommons.org/licenses/by-nc-nd/4.0/), which permits any noncommercial use, sharing, distribution and reproduction in any medium or format, as long as you give appropriate credit to the original author(s) and the source, provide a link to the Creative Commons license and indicate if you modified the licensed material. You do not have permission under this license to share adapted material derived from this chapter or parts of it.

The images or other third party material in this chapter are included in the chapter's Creative Commons license, unless indicated otherwise in a credit line to the material. If material is not included in the chapter's Creative Commons license and your intended use is not permitted by statutory regulation or exceeds the permitted use, you will need to obtain permission directly from the copyright holder.

CHAPTER 7

What Japan Gained and Lost

Abstract The Japanese economy was not jump-started even after the bad loans were resolved. While Japan succeeded in averting the trade war escalating into a full diplomatic showdown and the banking crisis propagating into a systemic meltdown, its economic size and per capita income came to be overshadowed by its peers, particularly those in Asia. Japan tried to transform itself when its growth model reached an impasse in the mid-1980s, but the efforts resulted in bubbles, and the ensuing long clean-up process may have distracted the country from the critical task of developing a new growth model.

Keywords Financial surplus · Self-insurance · Stagnant investment · Growth path · Welfare growth · Social fabric

As shown in Fig. 7.1, the Japanese private non-financial corporate sector borrowed massively during the bubble years. During the in-between years, it did not borrow much in net but did not repay much either. Only after the crisis and following the three rounds of intensive bank inspections, the non-financial corporate sector started big repayments. Finally, the sector had shed off excess debts and stopped repaying in FY 2005 and 2006, but, in net, it did not start new investments either. Then there

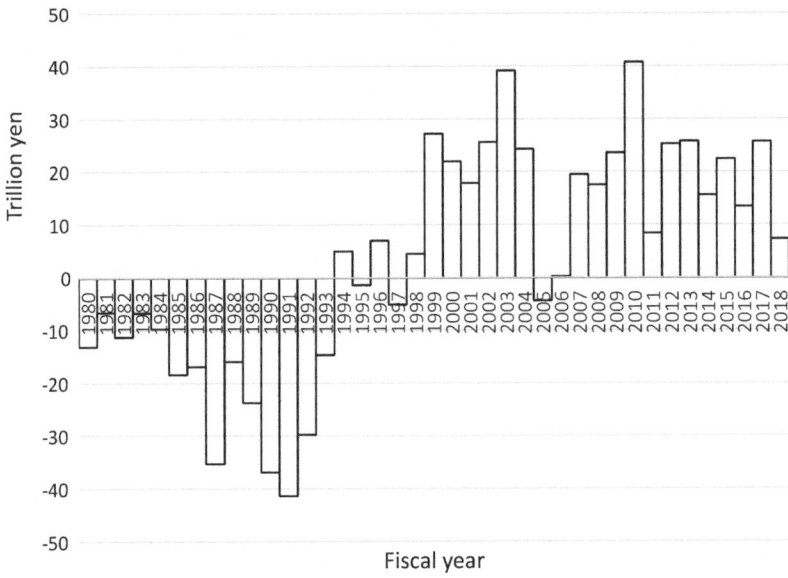

Fig. 7.1 Financial surplus/deficit of private non-financial corporates (*Source* Bank of Japan, Flow of funds statistics)

came the Global Financial Crisis in 2008 and the Great Eastern Earthquake and its tsunami and subsequent nuclear crisis in 2011, making the corporate Japan even more cautious. It continued to repay debts, and those companies which got no more debts to repay accumulated cash at hand. The Japanese corporate sector became a major net saver.

After main banks demonstrated that they may not necessarily be reliable in times of stress, borrowers resorted to self-insurance. As shown in Fig. 7.2, the corporate Japan rapidly reduced debts payable to banks after the 1998 banking crisis and piled on cash at hand after the Global Financial Crisis. The net bank debt (i.e., bank debt minus cash) shrank to only 7% of the total asset at the end of FY 2018. On the other hand, the equity to asset ratio, which long stayed below 20%, started to jump up after the banking crisis and reached 42% at the end of FY 2018. Private non-financial corporations transformed their balance sheets during the last two decades so that they rely less on banks and more on their own cash and capital.

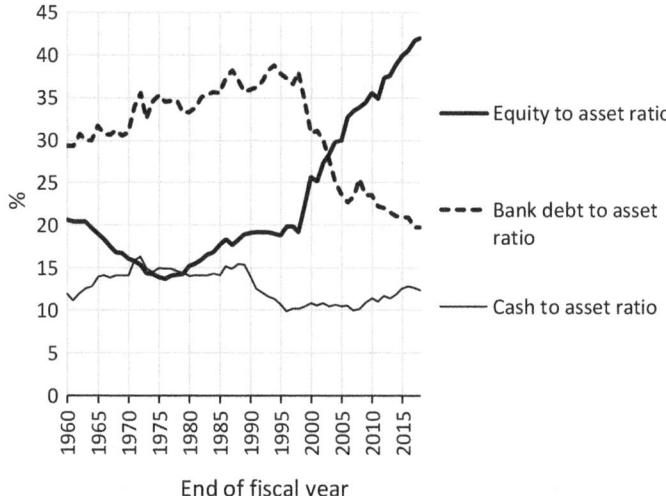

Fig. 7.2 Balance sheet composition of private non-financial corporations (*Note* Corporations of all size and all non-financial industries. Equity to asset ratio represents shareholders' equity [net worth] as percent of total assets. Bank debts represent loans payable to financial institutions. Cash represents cash and bank deposits held by corporations. *Source* Ministry of Finance, Financial Statements Statistics of Corporations, FY2018)

The corporate Japan's much-enhanced risk-taking capacity, however, did not result in increased investments. The contribution of increase in capital stock to the potential growth rate fluctuated between negative 0.7% and positive 0.6% (Fig. 7.3). The capital stock was not revamped to take advantage of the information and mobile technologies and became obsolete year by year. The contribution of the total factor productivity growth to the potential growth rate was well above 1% in early years of the 2000s but became almost nil toward the end of 2010s. It was expected in the early 2000s that, once the Japanese economy broke away from the yoke of the bad loans and excess debts, it could make a jump start. This expectation did not materialize. The potential growth rate never rose above the level experienced during the first lost decade.

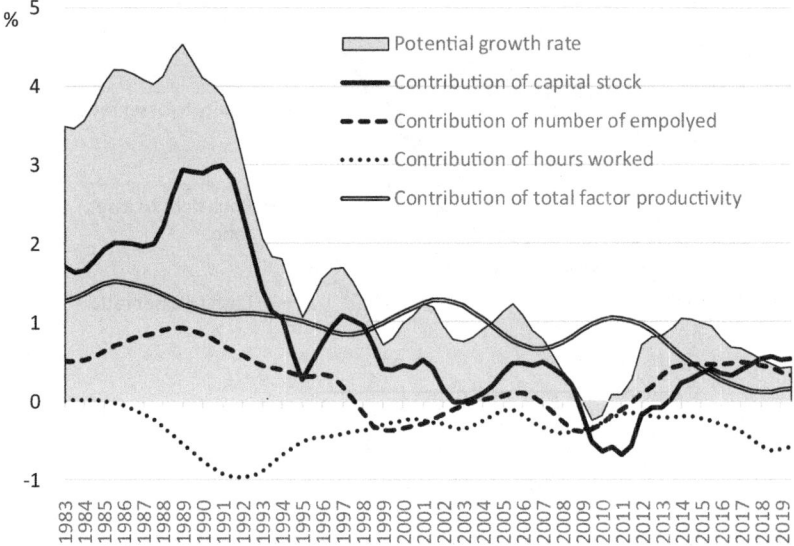

Fig. 7.3 Factor contributions to the potential growth rate (*Source* Bank of Japan, Output Gap and Potential Growth Rate, April 2020)

The relative economic clout of Japan, as measured by the GDP expressed in the current exchange rate, which in 1995 reached 71% of the United States, came down to one quarter in 2018 (Fig. 7.4, Panel A). It was ten times bigger than the Chinese economy in 1993 but was only 36% in 2018. The average living standard of a Japanese, as measured by the GDP per capita expressed in the purchasing power parity rate, was only 13% less than an average American's in 1991 but is 30% less now (Panel B). The Taiwanese overtook the Japanese already in 2009 and the Koreans have become almost as well off as the Japanese.

Abiad et al. (2014), five economists at the International Monetary Fund, look at medium-term output dynamics after 88 banking crisis episodes. With charts showing changes in real GDP per capita for the ten years leading to the crisis and seven years following the crisis, they persuasively categorized the postcrisis growth path into three types. The first group of crises, such as those in Japan in 1997 and Thailand in 1997, resulted in growth at persistently slower rate than before, and in addition to immediate output losses, ever wider deviation from the pre-crisis

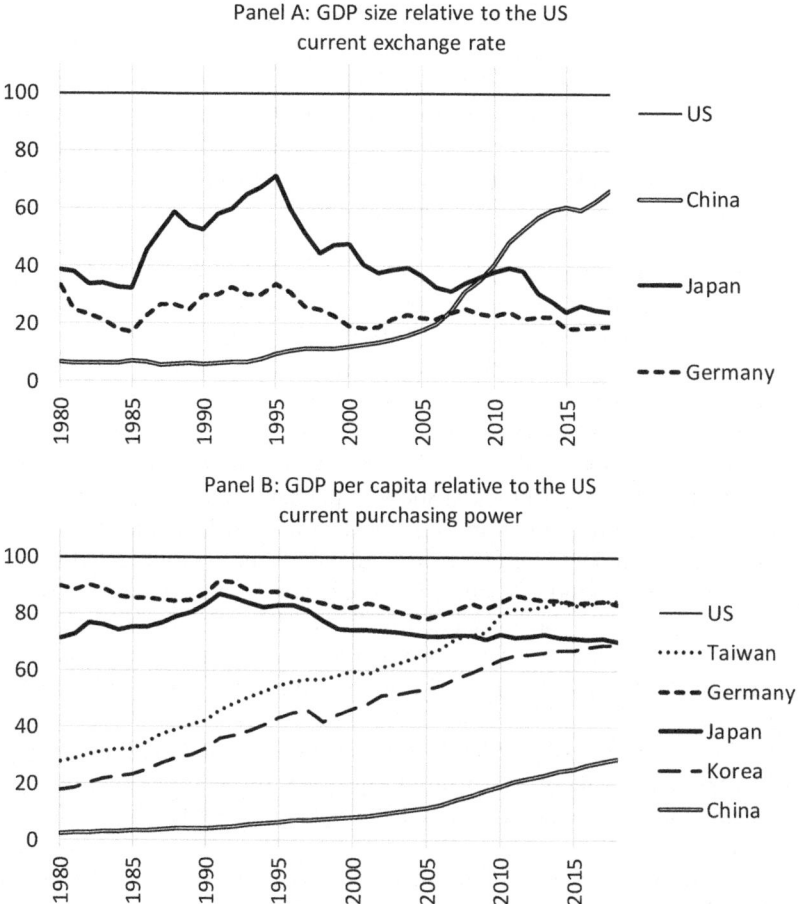

Fig. 7.4 Changes in the economic clout of countries and the living standard of nationals (*Source* World Bank, World Development Indicators database [for Panel A] and International Monetary Fund, World Economic Outlook Database [for Panel B])

trends. The second group, such as Korea in 1997 and Sweden in 1991, resulted in return to the pre-crisis growth rate, but the initial output losses are not recovered. The third group, such as Turkey in 2000 and Mexico in 1994, resulted in growth outperforming the pre-crisis trends.

Though Abiad et al. (2014) do not argue for this, one may tempted to infer from these cases that quick hard-landing reforms prescribed by the IMF (such as Korea in 1997 and Mexico in 1994) and quick and aggressive self-reforms (such as Sweden in 1991) can preserve or even improve medium-term growth, while the Japanese style soft-landing can leave lasting damages. Could Japan have belonged to the second or third group had the IMF imposed ruthless reforms?

But the growth paths look quite different if we include period before and after the 18 years examined by Abiad et al. (2014). In Japan (Fig. 7.5, Panel A), it was the burst of bubbles in 1990 which kinked the growth trend. The banking crisis in 1997–1998 did not result in a change in the growth trend and may be considered rather as an example of the second group characteristics. In Thailand (Panel B), the pre-crisis decade of sharp growth acceleration was rather a deviation from the long-term trend and the post-crisis period could be considered as a return to normalcy. Not shown in Fig. 7.5, but Indonesia shows a pattern similar to Thailand.

Looking at a short time horizon, Abiad et al. (2014) maintain that the crisis in Korea in 1997 resulted only in initial output loss and did not lower the growth trend. Despite the structural reforms done in the wake of the crisis, however, the growth gradually decelerated from around 2000 (Panel C) and the case may be considered as an example of the first group. Sweden in 1991 (Panel D) looks like an example of the third group rather than the second.

In short, the cases of Sweden in 1991, Turkey in 2000, and Mexico in 1994 may imply a merit of a painful big quick surgery, but the cases of Thailand, Indonesia, and Korea in 1997 may suggest that is not always the case.

The economic growth in the post-war Japan (Panel A) is characterized by three steady periods with two kinks. The post-war miracle growth kinked around the time of the hyperinflation ensuing the October 1973 oil crisis. The economy transited to a more moderate growth, and then kinked again at the burst of bubbles in the early 1990s. Since then, the Japanese economy maintained a slower but steady growth. The banking crisis in 1998 and the corporate and banking restructuring in 2001–2002 left scars much less noticeable than the one left by the Global Financial Crisis in 2008.

This structure of three steady periods and two kinks contrasts sharply with the US growth path (Panel G), which shows fluctuation around the steady trend only, as introductory economics textbook presupposes,

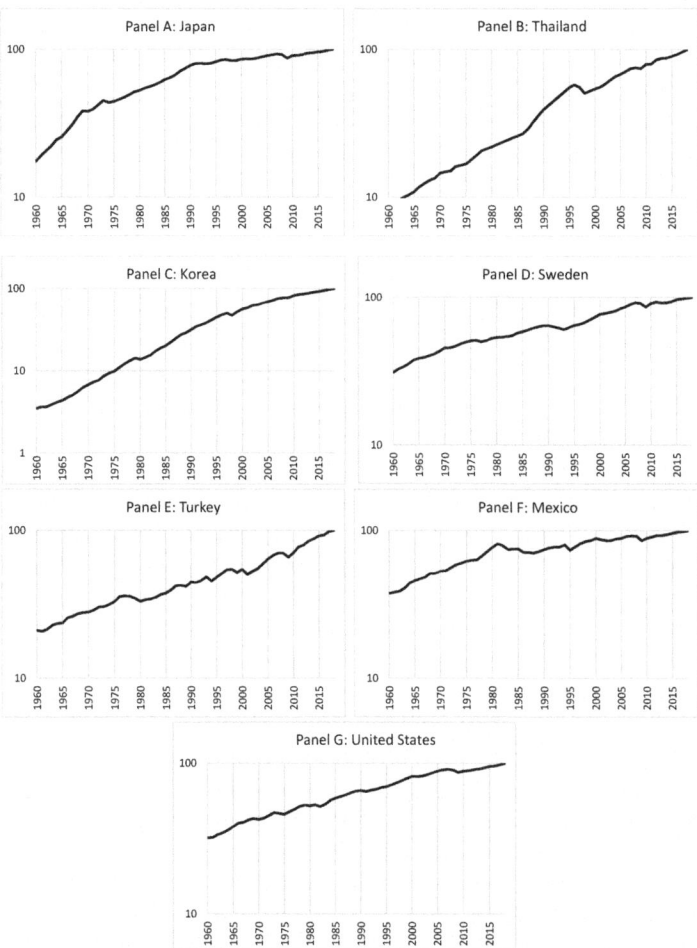

Fig. 7.5 Changes in real GDP per capita (The level in 2018 = 100) (*Note* The vertical axis is with logarithmic scale. Korea, whose growth during the period is by far the biggest, is shown with different scale. *Source* World Bank, World Development Indicators database)

until the Global Financial Crisis caused a modest downward change in the growth trend. Though not shown, the UK growth path is similar to the US one.

The steadiness of the Japanese growth since the second kink, in spite of all the dramas described in this report, may make one suspect that the bubbles and the busts may have been part of the adjustment process resulting from transition from one growth model to another. The transition might have been necessitated by factors such as demographic changes (Japan transited from the period with demographic bonus to that with demographic onus in the early 1990s) and the size of the Japanese economy becoming excessive to be sustained by the export-led growth strategy.

In Chapter 1, we called Japan's rapid modernization in the late nineteenth and early twentieth centuries as its first miracle and the post-WWII growth as the second. Japan sustained the second miracle by transforming its growth engine from reconstruction to export, from cheap and abundant labor to capital-intensive plants then to advanced technologies, and from energy dependent production processes to energy efficient ones of the post-oil shock era.

When the existing growth model reached an impasse in the mid-1980s, Japan did try to transform itself again, from the world's factory to the world's headquarters, investor, and financial center, from a country of workaholic to an attractive land with new lifestyles, and from a selfish beneficiary of the world order to a contributor to global commons, as we saw in Chapter 2. But the new visions and dreams that were quickly fabricated in the latter half of the 1980s largely turned out to be papier-mâché and resulted in an inefficient allocation of resources. Massive costs were incurred to banks, corporations, and the government, and burdens were imposed on the labor force, as Chapters 3–6 described.

But perhaps more significant were the lost opportunities. Japan already confronted with the need to design a new system which can support a new growth model in the mid-1980s, as well recognized by the Mayekawa report, but spend the 1990s mainly to prevent the collapse of the old system. The crisis in 1998 made the failure of the old system evident, and immediately after that, the Economic Planning Agency (1999), in its report approved by the Cabinet, clearly defined the task as follows:

The system which supported the growth of the Japanese economy till the 1980s relied on banks' corporate governance functions under the mainbank system and other established practices. The approach was effective during the catch-up period, as the key success factors in the period were piecemeal improvements in production efficiency and in products. Japan, however, completed the catch-up processes which can be attained by piecemeal improvements and is now being caught-up by emerging competitors. Now, the key success factors are the abilities to innovate and propose new lifestyles for an affluent society and excavate new demands, but the existing system do not support activities to foster such success factors well.

As the Japanese economy needs to proactively face new challenges, it should take greater amount of risks. The key task here is designing a new system which can support economic agents to face forward-looking challenges without scaring the households. So far, the Japanese household sector has been protected from risks, but this is just because banks absorbed enormous risks backed by the growing value of the real estate collaterals and large latent gains on the equities held, not because of the excellence in risk diversification system embedded in the Japanese economy.

We should design a new system where i) risks can be assumed in a well-diversified manner and are compensated by proper returns, ii) economic agents proactively face new challenges to innovate technologies and life styles, and iii) returns on financial investments are improved.

The task was defined clearly in 1999, but Japan spent the first half of the 2000s to clean up the mess created by the old system.

A new system would require many new components which are complementary to each other: A governance framework that can effectively allocate risk, return, and monitoring function within the society; a growth model that can create values by solving the problems the global community confronts with; a social norm that can foster entrepreneurship and innovation while preserving social fabric; properly designed safety nets; and vibrant investments. The transformation requires enormous efforts, courage, resources, and ingenuities of business leaders, policymakers, and all other members of the society. The 1986–2004 financial cycle distracted the country from this critical task to transform itself.

The slow GDP growth does not necessarily mean that Japan lagged in all aspects of public welfare. Jones and Klenow (2016), who propose a summary statistics for economic well-being of people in a country, argue that, despite its "lost decades" after 1990, Japan moves sharply up in the growth rankings when considering welfare instead of income. According to them, both Japan and the United States had average annual income growth just over 2.0% between 1980 and 2007, a period which includes the Japanese crisis but not the Global Financial Crisis. But Japan's annual welfare growth nearly doubled to 4.0% when rising life expectancy, rising consumption relative to GDP, and rising leisure are incorporated, almost one percentage point above the US welfare growth rate of 3.1%.

The rising leisure is expressed as the constant negative contribution of work hours to the potential growth rate in Fig. 7.3. Figure 7.6 shows male and female longevity in Japan, which ever improves without any kinks and outperforms Germany and the United States by wide margins.

Japan may not have used the 1986–2004 financial cycle most efficiently to find and establish a new growth model. But Japan evaded a full-fledged trade war in the 1980s and, despite the burst of bubbles two to three times bigger than those in the United States in the 2000s, averted a meltdown of its banking system in the 1990s and 2000s. Through a painful

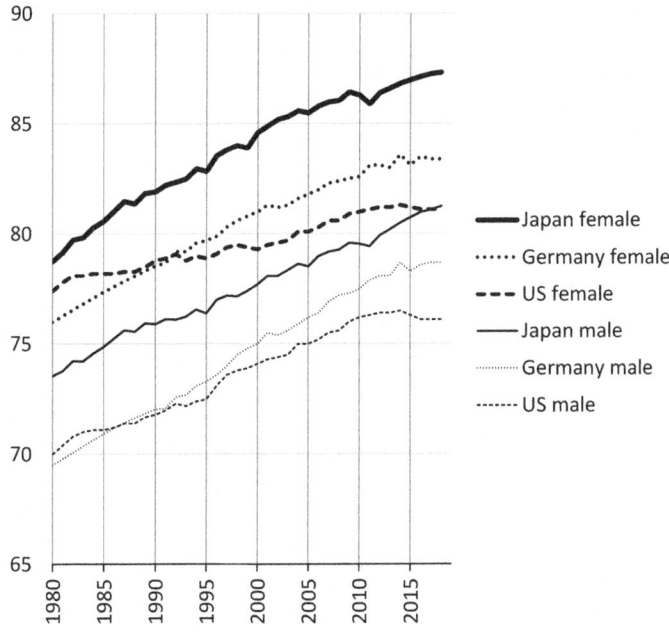

Fig. 7.6 Male and female life expectancy at birth in Germany, Japan, and the United States (*Source* World Bank, World Development Indicators Database)

process, it acquired a toolbox to deal with distress in the banking and corporate sectors.

In Japan today, streets are clean, trains operate punctually, and people are largely polite and diligent. Populist overtone is reasonably contained. Shared norms often work more effectively than coercion. The country may be assessed to have maintained its basic social fabric, which should constitute the foundation of any third miracle to come.

References

Abiad, A., Balakrishnan, R., Brooks, P. K., Leigh, D., & Tytell, I. (2014). What's the damage? Medium-term output dynamics after financial crises. In S. Claessens, A. Kose, L. Laeven, & F. Valencia (Eds.), *Financial crises: Causes, consequences, and policy responses* (pp. 277–307). International Monetary Fund.

Economic Planning Agency. (1999). *Annual report on the Japanese economy: Challenges to be met to resurrect the economy (Nennji Keizai Houkoku: Keizai saisei eno chousen)*.

Jones, C. I., & Klenow, P. J. (2016). Beyond GDP? Welfare across countries and time. *American Economic Review, 106*(9), 2426–2457.

Open Access This chapter is licensed under the terms of the Creative Commons Attribution-NonCommercial-NoDerivatives 4.0 International License (http://creativecommons.org/licenses/by-nc-nd/4.0/), which permits any noncommercial use, sharing, distribution and reproduction in any medium or format, as long as you give appropriate credit to the original author(s) and the source, provide a link to the Creative Commons license and indicate if you modified the licensed material. You do not have permission under this license to share adapted material derived from this chapter or parts of it.

The images or other third party material in this chapter are included in the chapter's Creative Commons license, unless indicated otherwise in a credit line to the material. If material is not included in the chapter's Creative Commons license and your intended use is not permitted by statutory regulation or exceeds the permitted use, you will need to obtain permission directly from the copyright holder.

Index

Symbols
2-year and 3-year rule, 85, 86
50% and 80% rule, 86

A
administrative guidance, 29, 53, 73
Aoki Masahiko, 92
Ashikaga Bank, 90
Asian financial crisis, 74

B
bad loans, 49, 85
bail-in, 78
Bankers' Association, 55
Bank for International Settlements, 35
Banking Bureau of the Ministry of Finance, 53
Banking Law, 16
Bank of Japan, 11, 13, 28, 37, 54, 56, 66, 75, 99
Bank resolution, 89
Basel Committee on Banking Supervision (BCBS), vii
Basel II, vii

Bernanke, Ben, 35, 36
Black Monday, 35
blanket deposit protection, 100
Board of Governors of the Federal Reserve System, 13, 29, 34, 37
Borio, Claudio, 2, 35
bubbles, 19
Byres, Wayne, i, 7

C
Catch 22, 50
Caterpillar Inc., 15
China, 2
Civil Rehabilitation Law, 94
civil responsibility, 78
cleaning, 36
Columbia Pictures, 23
construction industry, 18, 100
Containing Japan, 24
Cooperative Credit Purchasing Corporation, 5
Corporate Reorganization Act, 94
Council on Economic and Fiscal Policy, 75
credit cooperative, 60

credit crunch, 74
criminal responsibility, 78
cross-shareholding, 51

D
debt overhang, 91, 101
déjà vu, 5
demographic onus, 112
Department of the Treasury, 15, 79
Deposit Insurance Corporation of Japan (DICJ), 16, 54, 98
Deposit Insurance Law, 54, 90
deposit insurance limit, 16
deregulation, 16
Diet, 57, 99
disclosure, 16, 71
discount cash flow approach, 88
distribution industry, 100

E
equal opportunity menace, 3
European Central Bank, 77
export-led growth strategy, 9, 112

F
false deposit certificates, 49
Federal Reserve Bank of New York, 34
financial cycle, 2
Financial Reconstruction Commission, 69, 71, 102
Financial Services Agency (JFSA), vii, 7, 85, 87, 102
Financial Stability Board (FSB), vii, 78
Financial Supervisory Agency (JFSA), 68, 72, 102
Financial System Planning Bureau of the Ministry of Finance, 102
Financial Times, 49, 66
Fiscal Investment and Loan Program, 75
fiscal policy, 34
Fisher, Irving, 78
Focused Inspection, 85
forward guidance, 75
Fourth National Comprehensive Development Plan, 12

G
G7 Summit, 14
Galbraith, John Kenneth, 6, 35
Geithner, Timothy, 79
Glass-Steagall, 67
global city, 6, 12
Global Financial Crisis, 5, 78, 95, 106, 110
Global Financial Partnership Center (GLOPAC), 7
Gomi Hirofumi, 73, 86, 89
Great Depression, 34
Great Eastern Earthquake, 106
Greek tragedies, 5
Group of Five (G5), 10
Guidelines for Multi-Creditor Out-of-Court Workout, 94

H
Hamanaka Hideichiro, 72
Himino Ryozo, vii, 3, 40
Hino Masaharu, 73
Hokkaido Takushoku Bank, 58, 65

I
in-between years, 47
income inequality, 97
Indonesia, 77, 110
Industrial Bank of Japan, 92
Industrial Revitalization Corporation of Japan (IRCJ), 93

Inspection Manual, 85
International Monetary Fund, 77, 78, 110
Inui Fumio, 73

J
Japanese employment system, 95
Japanese Government Bond (JGB), 75
job-search ice age, 96, 101
Jusen, 51, 57, 66

K
Kajiyama Seiroku, 64, 68
Kaminsky, Graciela, 15
Kanemaru Shin, 29
keiretsu, 67
Korea, 109

L
Land-Holding Tax, 33
land policy, 34, 43
land price, 28
leaning, 36
Lehman Brothers, 5, 77
Liberal Democratic Party, 29, 64, 68
lifetime employment, 96
loan servicers, 93
longevity, 114
Long-Term Credit Bank Act, 67
Long-Term Credit Bank of Japan (LTCB), 66
loss compensation, 49
Louvre Accord, 13

M
main bank system, 92
Mayekawa Haruo, 11
Mayekawa Report, 11, 112
Mexico, 109

Mieno Yasushi, 28, 54, 55
Minister for Economic Planning, 28
Minister for Financial Services, 86
Minister of Finance, 10, 11, 13, 15, 28, 66, 69
Ministry of Finance, 15, 29, 52, 54, 66, 76, 99
Minsky moment, 2
min-katsu, 12
Mitsubishi Bank, 18
Miyazawa Kiichi, 11, 54, 64, 99
monetary policy, 13, 28
Moody's Investor Service, 75
moral hazard, 78, 102
Mori Nobuchika, 80
Mussa, Michael, 36
Myers, Stewart, 91

N
Nakai Hisao, 64
Nakai Sei, 44, 65
Nakaso Hiroshi, 63
Nakasone Yasuhiro, 10, 11
National Land Agency, 31
National Land Utilization Law, 34
negative feedback loops, 79
Nippon Credit Bank, 69
non-bank lenders, 19
non-recurring losses, 97
non-regular employees, 97
Northern Rock, 5

O
Obuchi Keizo, 68
oil crisis, 110
Okita Saburo, 10
on-the-job training, 97, 101
Osaka Stock Exchange, 2, 22
Otto von Bismarck, 73

P
Paulson, Henry, 5
Pilgrim Fathers, 72
Plaza Accord, 10
potential growth rate, 107
President of the United States, 10, 11, 14
Prime Minister, 10, 11, 14, 31, 54, 68, 69, 73, 75, 86
prompt corrective action, 71
provisioning, 69, 71
prudential policy, 29
purchase and assumption approach (P&A), 16, 54, 57, 59

Q
Quantitative Restriction Circular (QR), 30, 42
queues of depositors, 5, 63

R
Rajan, Raghuram, 9
Reagan, Ronald, 11
real estate industry, 17, 20, 24, 100
regular employees, 97
Reinhart, Carmen, 3, 15
Resolution and Collection Corporation (RCC), 93
Resona Bank, 88, 90
Resort Development Law, 13
resort towns, 13
reverse Minsky moment, 2, 89
Rockefeller Center, 23
Rogoff, Kenneth, 3
Rubin Doctrine of International Finance, 79

S
Sanyo Securities, 5, 58
Second World War, 1
Secretary of the Treasury, 13, 15, 79
Securities and Exchange Commission, 71
seniority-based wage, 96
Shiga Sakura, 73
shinkin bank, 60
Showa Financial Crisis, 52
SME Business Rehabilitation Support Co-operatives, 94
social fabric, 115
Special Inspection, 86, 88
Specialized Housing Finance Company (*Jusen*), 51, 57, 66
Standing Committee on Supervisory and Regulatory Cooperation (SRC), vii
Sumita Satoshi, 11, 28
Sumitomo Bank, 18, 92
Super SIV, 5
Suzuki Tsuneo, 67
Sweden, 109
systemic meltdown, 101

T
Takemori Shunpei, 89
Takenaka Heizo, 86, 89, 90
Takeshita Noboru, 10, 12
Tankan survey, 32, 80
tax policy, 33, 43
Taylor rule, 14, 39
Teikoku Bank, 92
temporary nationalization, 69
Thailand, 108
Tokyo Metropolitan Government, 12
Tokyo Prosecutors' Office, 66
Tokyo Stock Exchange, 2, 22, 55
too little, too late, 36
total factor productivity, 107
trade surplus, 23
trade war, 10
Troubled Asset Relief Program, 5
Turkey, 109

U

Ueda Kenichi, 7
unconventional monetary policy, 75
unemployment rate, 96
United Kingdom, 112
United States, 110
Universal Pictures, 23
unviable firms, 91, 101
US-Japan Ad Hoc Group on Yen/Dollar Exchange Rate, 15

V

VAT, 74
Vice Minister of Finance, 55, 66
Volcker, Paul, 10

W

welfare growth, 114
White, William, 35, 36
work hours, 114
wrong-way risk, 20

Y

yakuza, 23, 48
Yamaichi Securities, 58
Yanagisawa Hakuo, 86, 89, 90
yen, 10, 23, 28, 39, 75

Z

zero interest rate policy (ZIRP), 75
zombie firms, 88, 102

The manufacturer's authorised representative in the EU is Springer Nature Customer Service Centre GmbH, Europaplatz 3, 69115 Heidelberg, Germany. If you have any concerns regarding our products, please contact ProductSafety@springernature.com

Printed and bound by CPI Group (UK) Ltd, Croydon, CR0 4YY
23/03/2026
02076447-0006